KIRSTIE'S
REAL KITCHEN

Dedication

To my mum – I miss you every day – and to all those who think they can't cook.
If I can, anyone can, and it's much more fun than you think.

KIRSTIE'S
REAL KITCHEN

KIRSTIE ALLSOPP

Photography by Rita Platts

HODDER &
STOUGHTON

First published in Great Britain in 2017 by Hodder & Stoughton
An Hachette UK company

1

A CIP catalogue record for this title is available from the British Library

Hardback ISBN 978 1 473 6 4336 9
eBook ISBN 978 1 473 6 4337 6

Colour origination by Born Group
Printed and bound by Firmengruppe APPL, aprinta druck, Wemding, Germany

Hodder & Stoughton policy is to use papers that are natural, renewable and recyclable products and
made from wood grown in sustainable forests. The logging and manufacturing processes are expected to
conform to the environmental regulations of the country of origin.

Editorial Director: Nicky Ross
Editor: Susan Fleming
Project Editor: Patricia Burgess
Art Director and Designer: nic&lou
Photographer: Rita Platts
Home Economist: Emma Marsden
Senior Designer: Sarah Christie
Senior Production Controller: Susan Spratt

Hodder & Stoughton Ltd
Carmelite House
50 Victoria Embankment
London EC4Y 0DZ

www.hodder.co.uk

Contents

This book is about my journey towards cooking as a passionate traveller, as a pretty miserable, single twenty-something, as a new girlfriend, a terrified stepmother, then a new mother, and as a crafter learning new things in front of impatient TV cameras. It was a journey that brings me to now, when cooking is how I relax and what I love to do when I am not working.

The recipes in this book are what I cook day in and day out for my children and stepchildren, for my partner Ben, for our friends and family, for breakfast, lunch and dinner. They are not organised in the standard way – starters, main courses and puddings. Instead their arrangement reflects the way in which I have made my cooking journey – through making breakfasts for assorted family and guests, through finding the easiest way of feeding crowds of people at parties, through cooking teas and suppers for recalcitrant children. Even all these years later, I am still finding my way with the last of these, but I have learnt a few tricks, and some of my ideas may help those of you who are faced with a fussy eater.

Ben and I love entertaining, whether in London or at our home in Devon. We have lots of big dishes that we turn to for feeding crowds at parties; we have Sunday lunches that last until teatime; and we love Christmas, which we throw ourselves into and celebrate with all the bells and whistles. We are also very keen on cooking and eating outside, and Ben is a dab hand at barbecuing. Social occasions also allow me to indulge in one of my favourite hobbies – making cocktails. They ensure any gathering goes with a swing, so do try some of the recipes, both old and new, in the final chapter.

Cooks always talk about their food influences, often their mothers or grandmothers. I adored my mother, and her early death from breast cancer is the greatest loss of my life so far. She was an inspiration and brilliant at entertaining, but she was not one of my food influences. Oddly, someone I've never met – my great-great grandmother, Minnie, Lady Hindlip – has influenced me more in terms of food. That's because I happened to come across a signed copy of the cookbook she published in 1933. It offers a fascinating insight to life back then, but some of her recipes definitely stand the test of time and are included in this book.

I firmly believe that you can find the cook in yourself at any age. Being brought up in a microwave household does not mean you have to pass that legacy onto your children. Fundamentally, the reason for my learning to cook, and for writing this book, is that I want my children and stepchildren to cook. I want this because food is life, and life is lived better if we know what goes into our meals and take an interest in it. I very much hope you will enjoy what's served within these pages.

Kirstie Allsopp

MAY 2017

Chapter 1

Breakfast

When I spent time in Turkey during my youth, I acquired a taste for toast with tomatoes, soft cheese and rose jam for breakfast. (I love the combination of cheese and jam – think of Manchego and membrillo.) The Turkish version is probably still my favourite breakfast, closely followed by the scrambled eggs and smoked salmon we tend to have on Christmas morning. However, I also have a penchant for a masala omelette, replete with pepper, onion, chilli, coriander and my beloved ginger.

Breakfast time is quite busy in my house. On weekdays I can be making three or four different breakfasts every morning – a rod I have made for my own back, I readily admit. Whilst not all cereals are full of sugar, they are something of a treat food in our house. The boys do occasionally get cornflakes, or Rice Krispies with a bit of drinking chocolate sprinkled over the milk, but I am tough with them if they pour too much syrup over their toast or pancakes. I know everyone is bored with hearing that sugar is the devil's work, but I'm afraid it's true and we have to face up to it. In an effort to steer my kids away from sweet stuff, I make sure fresh fruit and plain yoghurt are always available, but I generally end up cooking something, which I don't mind at all. French toast, for instance, is quick, popular and it gets some egg into the boys.

At weekends we often have friends to stay, so once more there are different breakfasts to provide. The boys will probably come down at about 8am and want pancakes (their weekend treat); the guests will be more civilised and appear at around 9am, which is when, after they have had some fruit – or porridge, I often do that – I might start making the eggs, poached or scrambled. The Aga oven will have been busy cooking the tomatoes (see page 22) and the dry-cured, usually back, bacon. I like New York-style thin bacon best – I love butchers who cut bacon rashers to order – and it is best cooked on a rack in a pan in the roasting oven of the Aga (or under a grill). It cooks very quickly both ways, so turn it over and keep an eye on it. Crisp bacon with baked tomatoes and an egg, plus some good toast, makes a fine breakfast.

As eggs are rich in protein, vitamins and minerals, I like the boys to have an egg a day, and I am fairly good at organising that, particularly at breakfast. They like boiled eggs occasionally, with buttered soldiers; they will sometimes accept fried, scrambled or poached, but I often hide the eggs in other offerings, which might be a bit sneaky, but works. Oscar, for instance, loves mangoes, his favourite thing in the world. During the Alphonso mango season (from April to early July), we peel the fruit, remove the stone and purée the flesh with plain yoghurt. When he is not looking, I add an egg. It doesn't alter the flavour, just adds goodness. Similarly, my stepson Hal does a lot of competitive riding, which means he has to get up very early in the morning. What I do for him then is make a smoothie containing almonds, pear, avocado, some yoghurt, a soft banana perhaps (he's the only one who will eat them uncooked), plus an egg if I can get away with it. The smoothie is very white, which Hal likes, and it is a brilliant way of keeping him going.

Poached eggs

We were a scrambled egg and fried egg family until Ben taught me how to poach. Now I poach eggs a lot, but only because of my boiling-water tap. If I were offered the choice between an expensive handbag and my tap, I would always choose the latter. It is so useful.

Serves 4

4 eggs, at room temperature
fine salt
2–3 tbsp white wine or cider vinegar

I take a large saucepan to my boiling-water tap, fill it half-full, then add a pinch or two of salt and the vinegar. (This slightly affects the taste, but quickly helps to set the proteins in the egg white, which is what you want.) I then crack an egg into a cup or ramekin and slide it gently and carefully into the boiling water. The egg will set immediately on the outside, with little 'fraying', but I then move the pan to the hot plate of the Aga for just a minute or two more – I want the yolk still to be runny.

In the absence of a boiling-water tap or an Aga, bring a saucepan of water to the boil, add a pinch or two of salt and pour in the vinegar. Turn down the heat to slightly simmering. Break an egg into a cup or ramekin, then slide it into the pan where the water is actually bubbling and poach for about 3 minutes. There might be bits of stray egg white with this method, so remove them with a slotted spoon.

The chef Bill Granger, a master with eggs, has an entirely different way of poaching. He puts 5cm of water in a frying pan and brings it to the boil. He then turns off the heat and breaks the eggs carefully into the water. Lid on the pan, and the eggs are left to poach for 3 minutes.

Whichever method is used, remove the eggs from the water using a slotted spoon and dry briefly on a wad of kitchen paper. Serve immediately.

Eggs Benedict

This recipe is heavily influenced by the chef Bill Granger, whose restaurant in Notting Hill is a favourite of ours. He has also become a friend, as he is a fellow parent at the boys' school. I met him, and saw him cooking, when I went to a demo he was doing for charity. His hollandaise works every time (as long as I don't get over-confident and ignore the recipe), and I serve it with eggs, ham, smoked salmon or spinach. However, I eat it only very rarely now, as a treat, because it contains a huge amount of butter.

The classic Benedict recipe has ham under the eggs, but I sometimes put my favourite buttered spinach in there instead. You could also substitute smoked salmon for the ham (hollandaise is wonderful with fish). For additional flavour, add some chopped chives to the hollandaise, or a dusting of cayenne for a touch of spice.

Serves 4

4 eggs
2 English muffins
4 slices of ham

FOR THE HOLLANDAISE SAUCE
3 egg yolks
1 tbsp lemon juice
1 tbsp water
175g unsalted butter, freshly melted
salt and freshly ground white pepper

Start with the hollandaise. You can make it by hand, but it is so much easier in a processor, a technique Bill Granger taught me. Put the egg yolks, lemon juice and water in a food processor and blend until smooth. With the motor still running, slowly add the warm butter and keep processing until the sauce is thick and glossy. Season to taste with salt and pepper, and keep warm until needed. Be careful, as the sauce could split if 'warm' is too warm.

Meanwhile, poach the eggs (see page 14).

Halve and toast the muffins. Put a muffin half on each plate, and top with a slice of ham and a poached egg. Pour the hollandaise sauce generously over the egg, and serve immediately.

Herb omelette

I cook omelettes all the time and, a source of great joy to me, everyone in the house will eat an omelette! When we arrive back in London from Devon on a Sunday night, that's what I cook as a quick supper. I am a great one for chucking things in an omelette – cheese, tomatoes and potatoes (these last two cooked a little first), anything that is handy. The result might not look very tidy, but as far as taste is concerned, I haven't had a failure yet.

There are several wonderful gadgets on the market that can make your omelette-making even easier. Some are electric, with variously shaped containers: you put the beaten egg in, along with additions, close the lid and the omelette is made in minutes. Some containers are made especially for the microwave. I generally use a hinged double-omelette pan that I bought in Italy. I heat both pans on the Aga, put the beaten egg in one of them and quickly top with some herbs, lightly cooked tomatoes or finely grated cheese. When the underside is lightly browned, I put the other pan on top and flip it over to cook the other side. I then decant this perfectly round omelette onto a plate.

Serves 1–2, depending on appetite

3 large free-range eggs
knob of unsalted butter
1 tsp olive oil
3 tbsp chopped fresh herbs (chives, parsley, basil
   or marjoram, or a mixture of them all)
salt and freshly ground black pepper

Break the eggs into a bowl, season with salt and pepper and whisk together.

Melt the butter and oil together in an omelette pan or small frying pan over a medium to high heat. When the butter has melted, add the egg mixture. As the base begins to set, use a fork to draw the cooked mixture in from the side. This allows the uncooked egg to run underneath and start to set in turn. Continue doing this until the underside has set but is still soft on top.

Scatter the omelette with the herbs, fold it in half and carefully slide onto a warmed plate.

Scrambled eggs

Have you noticed that the scrambled eggs you see on hotel buffets are usually like leather? That's because they have been sitting for far too long. The most important thing to be aware of when cooking scrambled eggs is that the person you are cooking for must be waiting for them, not the other way around. (I have not managed to teach Ben this; at weekends he's often wandering around the house at the critical point.) My dad taught me how to make scrambled eggs, and I well remember him standing over me at the stove as I gradually learnt how to season, stir and scramble.

Flavourings can be added to the eggs just before serving: try chopped fresh herbs (chives are good), a spice, or some chilli if you like heat. Top with anything you like – fried bacon pieces, smoked salmon, shavings of Parmesan. Serve the eggs on a base of good toasted bread, a baked puff pastry square or circle, a bed of freshly wilted spinach, a fried or baked Portobello mushroom ... basically, whatever springs to mind.

Per person

2 large eggs
5g butter
salt and freshly ground black pepper

Crack the eggs into a bowl, season to taste with salt and pepper and whisk together.

Melt the butter in a suitable pan. When it is sizzling, turn the heat down to very low and add the beaten egg. Stir slowly with a wooden spoon, bringing the egg from the sides of the pan into the middle. The eggs will be ready when they are still slightly runny. Remove from the heat immediately, as they will continue to cook off the heat.

Just before spooning onto a warm plate or a slice of toast, add any extra flavourings (see my suggestions in the introduction above). Serve straight away.

Breakfast tomatoes

Almost every weekend we have cooked tomatoes for breakfast, which are easy to do in the oven while I am poaching or scrambling eggs.

- I put halved tomatoes in an ovenproof dish that can go straight to the table, and chuck in a little olive oil, salt, pepper, a few dashes of soy sauce and Worcestershire sauce, plus some grated garlic and chilli flakes to taste. This goes in the Aga for 10–15 minutes (about 200°C/Fan 180°C/Gas 6 in a conventional oven). I then serve it with sourdough toast, eggs and, if it's the weekend, some bacon. Ben likes a little Parmesan grated over his tomatoes.

- Sometimes, but not as often as I'd like, we have some leftover cooked tomatoes from breakfast. When they have cooled, I give them a taste and sometimes add a little olive oil and cider vinegar and pop them in the fridge. At lunchtime I then have an incredibly versatile extra to put with anything. Try cooking up some brown rice (I do mine in our old rice cooker), with salt, pepper, a tablespoon of coconut oil and the requisite amount of water. Obviously, you can cook the rice in a pan in the normal way. When ready, drain the rice and put it in a pretty serving bowl. Once it has cooled a bit, toss with the leftover tomatoes, followed by small cubes of feta cheese. A good lunchtime salad.

New York pancakes

American pancakes are smaller and thicker than the crêpe-like pancakes we usually have in the UK, and not as thick as drop scones. My children prefer the pancakes they can wrap around fillings, but then they are odd sometimes.

The recipe below is a more sophisticated version of the pancakes I throw together at the weekend, when I usually pour milk into a bowl, add two eggs (for two children) or three eggs for more, and whisk them together. I then sprinkle in plain flour until I get the consistency I want.

Makes 8–12 pancakes, depending on size

250g self-raising flour
good pinch of salt
4 medium eggs, separated

240ml milk
large knob of butter

Sift the flour and salt into a bowl and make a well in the centre. Add the egg yolks and milk to the well, then whisk the flour into the liquid, gradually drawing it in, until you have a smooth batter.

In a separate, very clean bowl, whisk the egg whites until foamy – you don't want them stiff. Using a large metal spoon, fold them into the batter – they add airiness and lighten the pancakes.

Heat a large frying pan over a medium heat. Add a little of the butter, enough to grease most of the surface of the pan. When it starts to foam, add large tablespoonfuls of the batter, leaving a space between them. Cook for a few minutes, until light brown on the underside and starting to set on the top. Flip them over and cook for another minute or so, until the second side is golden brown. Wrap them in a clean tea towel to keep warm while you make the remaining pancakes, finishing up the butter and the batter.

Serve with the same sort of things you would offer with French Toast (see page 26). The pancakes could also be used as a base for Eggs Benedict (see page 16), or even served as canapés if you make them blini-sized. In this case, soured cream and smoked salmon or Gravadlax (see page 214) would make a good topping.

French toast

If you can get your kids to eat this, you are on easy street. It's not so much a recipe as a reminder that this super-simple, nutritious, anytime foodstuff exists. Whether as breakfast, snack or Sunday-night post-train pick-me-up, French toast is a default food in our house, like pancakes but without the effort. And if you serve it with some bacon on a pretty plate, it makes a cooked breakfast that will really impress any overnight guests.

Some recipes include milk, but I'm always keen on the kids getting as much egg as possible, so I use just eggs and a pinch of salt.

Serves 4

4 large eggs
pinch of salt
knob of butter
8 slices of bread

In a roomy bowl, beat the eggs together, adding a pinch of salt.

Make sure your frying pan is super-hot, then chuck in the knob of butter.

Dunk each slice of bread in the egg mixture, soaking both sides.

Before the butter in the pan goes brown, add the bread and fry on each side until golden brown.

Serve alone or with some sweetness. I have two takers for maple syrup, one for agave syrup (or golden syrup if I let him), and another for Nutella or chocolate spread.

Fried bananas

As we live in London Monday to Friday during the school term, eating out is quite normal for my kids. We live just a short distance from Portobello Road, where there is a huge selection of different foods available. When I was a child, though, eating out was a very special treat. It happened when I came to London at October half-term to do a spot of Christmas shopping with Mum, or when we went to the Chinese restaurant on the road between Hungerford and Marlborough. This was where I tasted my first banana fritter and realised that, much as I love fresh bananas, cooked ones offer a whole different level of bliss. It is lucky that I ended up with a man whose father was addicted to cooked bananas, and who inculcated a similar devotion to them in his son. In our family it's only fruit-loathing Bay who won't touch them; the rest of us can't get enough, and five out of six ain't bad.

This is barely a recipe, but as we eat so much of it – as breakfast, pudding, snack and even a hangover cure – I couldn't leave it out. There's no time when cooked banana doesn't hit the spot. I am not enough of a food scientist to fully understand why cooking a banana turns it into toffee, but it does. Serve by itself, or with yoghurt, toast, ice cream or whatever takes your fancy. But please, please never again throw out a banana; the browner the better.

Serves 3–6, depending on appetite

3 large ripe bananas
30g unsalted butter

Peel the bananas and cut them in half lengthways.

Melt the butter in a suitably sized frying pan and add the banana halves, cut-side down. Over a gentle heat, fry them for up to 6 minutes or so. Check every now and again that they are not burning, but otherwise you really just leave them to do their own thing.

When they are quite brown on the flat side, turn them over carefully (as they will be soft), and brown the rounded side. They take no longer than 10 minutes in total, but the heat must be low.

Many recipes have honey, syrup or sugar added to the pan at the last minute, but I think good bananas need no added sweetness. With the butter, they are delicious enough by themselves.

Damson jam

We all love this jam for breakfast on our hot buttered toast, and I'm really grateful that Victoria Cranfield taught me how to make it when I was entering the Devon County Show competition for cream teas. Damsons are very flavourful and high in pectin, a natural setting agent, so they make a terrific jam.

**Fills 8–9
450g jars**

2.7kg damsons
450ml orange juice
finely grated zest of 1 orange
2.7kg granulated sugar

Place a metal teaspoon and a couple of saucers in the freezer – you'll need these later to test for setting point. Also, sterilise 8 or 9 jam jars (see Tip below) and keep them in a low oven – they need to be hot when potting up.

Meanwhile, wash the damsons and remove the stalks. Put the fruit into a large stainless-steel saucepan, add the orange juice and zest, and cook over a medium heat until the fruit is soft. Stir occasionally, pushing the damsons against the side of the pan to release the stones. They will rise to the top and you can then remove them with a slotted spoon.

Once you're confident all the stones have been removed, add the sugar to the fruit and simmer, stirring occasionally, until the sugar has dissolved. Bring to the boil, stirring all the time, otherwise it will stick on the bottom. Boil for 2 minutes only.

Now test for setting point. Take the pan off the heat and put a teaspoonful of the jam on a chilled saucer. Allow to cool, then push with your finger. If it wrinkles, the jam is ready. If not, put the jam back on the boil for another 2 minutes, then test again with the second cold saucer.

When ready, carefully ladle the mixture into the hot jars, filling them close to the top. Place a waxed disc on the surface straight away, then seal and label.

⟩ TIP ⟨

To sterilise jars (and lids) heat them in the oven at its lowest setting for 30 minutes, or put them through the hottest cycle in the dishwasher.

Fruit salad

You can't go wrong with a fruit salad served in a pretty glass bowl. It's simplicity itself to make, and there's no need to make a sugar syrup: just steep the chopped fruit in orange or apple juice. Sometimes, though, it's nice to ring the changes, so here I offer a few ideas:

- At the weekends for breakfast, along with the tomatoes, toast and egg of choice, we always have a big bowl of chopped fruit and a big bowl of plain yoghurt. The fruit can be prepared the day before, as it doesn't really go off, and you don't have to worry about quantities because leftover fruit salad will always be eaten. Apart from the usual fruit bowl ingredients, try adding a few tropical touches, such as passionfruit, pineapple and kiwi – they add a zing that makes a great start to the day.

- If you don't finish the fruit salad at breakfast, you could have it for pudding later, perhaps with a little booze added. I like Calvados, St Germain elderflower liqueur or (my latest obsession) a rose liqueur we tasted at the Christmas Fair, but you can add anything you fancy. If serving fruit salad for pudding, I would offer bowls of cream or clotted cream on the table, as well as yoghurt, for people to help themselves.

- I like to include little cubes of apple, not chunks that are big enough to trip you up, and cubes of stone fruit, after stoning. I wouldn't add ripe peaches, nectarines or figs, as I prefer to eat those by themselves, and I am not fond of citrus in fruit salads. I often use things from the fruit bowl that look as though they wouldn't be picked up and eaten by someone without the brown bits being cut off. Once suitably trimmed, they are perfect for a salad.

Seville orange marmalade

This recipe has won Victoria Cranfield several awards, including the Great Taste Gold Award in 2006. Cranfield's, as it was, is now The Proper Marmalade Company, and in 2016 Victoria opened what might be the world's first marmalade shop, in Ilfracombe, north Devon.

Here the fruit is cooked whole because it makes the skin easier to cut. The amount of sugar used depends on the juice content of the fruit (see method).

Makes about 2.8kg or 8–9 jars

1kg Seville oranges
1 large unwaxed lemon
1.4 litres water
granulated sugar (have 2kg to hand)

First place a metal spoon and several saucers in the freezer. You'll need these later to test for setting point. Also set out about 9 sterilised jam jars (see page 29).

Meanwhile, wash the fruit to remove all dust and dirt. Seville orange skins are not treated, but lemons often are. If you can't get an unwaxed lemon, buy an ordinary one and scrub the skin in hot soapy water before rinsing well.

Put the whole fruit in a saucepan, lemons on the bottom, cover with the water and bring to the boil. Reduce to a simmer, then cover and cook for 20–30 minutes. Turn the fruit over so that the lemons are at the top but still submerged and simmer for a further 20 minutes. They are ready when a knife pierces the orange skin with little resistance.

Take the pan off the heat, keep the lid on, and allow to go cold, preferably overnight.

Keep all the cooking water. Cut the fruit in half and squeeze the flesh and juice into a large measuring jug or bowl. To do this, you can use an electric squeezer or scoop everything out with a spoon, using a fork to separate the pips. Add the pulp and juice to the cooking water, but discard all the pips.

Slice each half of orange skin in half again, then cut widthways into strips as thick or thin as you like. Add the strips to the reserved liquid and note the amount. For each 600ml of this mixture, you will need 450g sugar.

Return the prepared fruit mix to the saucepan and add the sugar. Simmer gently, stirring until the sugar has completely dissolved. Now turn up the heat and bring to a rolling boil. Boil for 25 minutes, stirring occasionally.

Take the pan off the heat and do your first test for a set. With the cold metal spoon, take a small sample of the liquid, dribble it onto a cold saucer, then place both spoon and saucer in the fridge for a few minutes. If the liquid wrinkles when nudged with your finger, the marmalade is ready. If not, return the pan to the heat and boil for just 5 minutes more. Put a clean spoon and in the freezer while this is happening. Test again on a clean cold saucer.

When ready, stir the marmalade, then let it stand in the pan for 15 minutes, which will ensure an even distribution of peel. A skin may start to form, but this can be stirred in before the next step.

Pot the rested marmalade into the sterilised jars and seal immediately. Remember to label and date.

Chapter 2

Salads
& Vegetables

I think there is something really special about eating vegetables that you have grown yourself. For a start, you know they have not been chemically enhanced in any way, and they will be fresher and tastier than anything you can find in a shop. (However, having said that, I am very lucky to live near one of the best greengrocers in west London, Michanicou, where the vegetables are top quality.) My sister-in-law Emily has an amazing allotment right in the middle of London, which she tends beautifully. She never has to buy vegetables, and for a number of years, while my father-in-law was still alive, her little plot produced more than enough to feed the whole family at a barbecue to celebrate his birthday.

I like eating vegetables, and recently made myself a courgette, broccoli and red pepper stir-fry for Sunday supper. It looked so pretty that I tweeted a pic of it and lots of people came back asking, 'What are you having it with?' It is a perversely British thing to see vegetables only as an accompaniment to something else. Often, as a family, we sit down to a meal consisting entirely of vegetables, and I think that this lies at the heart of healthy eating.

Like increasing numbers of people, I try to eat seasonally, using what is in the garden or what looks good in my local shop or supermarket. Of course, loads of fruit and veg are now imported from other countries, so it's possible to eat, say, strawberries or new potatoes, at any time of year. These may not be seasonal to us, but such imports do bring us a much wider choice. For instance, roast vegetables at one time in Britain would have consisted solely of roots, such as parsnips and carrots, but now we have a vast array of other delicious things, including peppers and aubergines, that can be roasted too (see my ideas on page 52).

I cook most of my vegetables in a way that is a little unusual. In an attempt to cut down on the use of oil, I use a minute amount of water instead. Try it and you will never go back to drowning greens in a panful of water. Have a jug of hot water at the side of the stove. Put some chopped-up garlic and chilli in your pan, add a little of the hot water and perhaps some salt. Cook for a moment or two until the water boils off, then add a little more water before adding some chopped-up veg, such as broccoli, carrots or asparagus. Boil off the water again, then add some flavourings, lemon for instance, and a bit more water, until the veg are cooked to your taste. If you cut carrots or courgettes into matchsticks (or spirals), they will cook in this way in a matter of seconds.

Salad is one of my favourite things, and probably what we eat most of from the garden, as we are generally at Grange, our home in Devon, during the summer months when lettuces are aplenty. There is a great salad dressing on page 60, but my own taste is for something much simpler. I tend to use tiny amounts of vinegar or lemon juice and oil, combining them half and half to make the dressing sharper. My current favourite thing, though, is to use tomatoes and their juices as a dressing, which works amazingly well (see page 59).

Carla's lentil, feta & coriander salad

If I'm filming, I am often away from home or have a very early start, and can't take the boys to school, so I really treasure the days when I can get on my Swifty Scooter and whizz down Ladbroke Grove behind my speed-freak sons. Once they are safely in school, I head to Tea's Me, a tiny café run by Carla, a Notting Hill legend. As well as running the café, Carla has been catering for every sort of event for years, including some parties of ours. This salad is one that goes down a storm, and I often make it now too: it's easy to prepare in advance, feeds the masses, is easy to serve and looks lovely. It also seems to last for a few days afterwards, which is fine by me, as I'm a great one for leftovers. Bless Carla for letting me include it in this book.

Serves 8

500g Puy lentils
2 bay leaves
125ml good-quality extra virgin olive oil
90ml lemon juice
salt and freshly ground black pepper
1 bunch each of fresh mint and coriander, leaves chopped

2 medium red onions, peeled, halved and thinly sliced
200g baby spinach leaves
400g good-quality feta cheese, cubed or crumbled

Put the lentils and bay leaves in a large pan, cover with boiling water and simmer for 20 minutes. Drain well, rinse in cold water, then drain thoroughly again.

Put the lentils in a large salad bowl, and add the olive oil and lemon juice, with salt and pepper to taste. Toss in the mint, coriander and red onions.

At the last moment, mix in the spinach leaves and small chunks of feta. Serve cold with delicious grilled bread.

Roasted mackerel salad

I would sooner give up chocolate, potatoes or cheese than be deprived of tomatoes. This is one of those brilliant recipes that, accompanied by rocket and followed by a tub of ice cream, makes a perfect sunny Saturday lunch. It comes via my friend Eloise. (She once stumbled across an S&M photo shoot in a cave on the beach near Meadowgate while walking the dog, but hasn't let that hold her back.)

Serves 6

500g cherry tomatoes
red wine vinegar and olive oil
6–12 fresh mackerel fillets, depending
  on appetite
handful of salad leaves
salt and freshly ground black pepper

FOR THE PICKLED SHALLOTS
2 tbsp caster sugar

100ml red wine vinegar
3 shallots, peeled and sliced 1mm thick

FOR THE HORSERADISH DRESSING
15g peeled fresh horseradish, finely
  grated
4 tbsp crème fraîche
3 tbsp extra virgin olive oil
1–1½ tbsp red wine vinegar

First make the pickled shallots: put the sugar and vinegar into a small saucepan and heat gently until the sugar has dissolved. Add the shallots and set aside to marinate while you put together the rest of the recipe.

Preheat the oven to 200°C/Fan 180°C/Gas 6. Put the tomatoes in a baking tray with a splash of red wine vinegar and olive oil and some salt and pepper. Roast until they have started to blister on top and the juices are becoming sticky, about 8–10 minutes. Once ready, they can be served at room temperature.

Brush the mackerel fillets with a little oil and season with salt and pepper. Heat a frying pan until hot over a medium heat, then pan-fry the fish skin-side down until it becomes crisp and golden, 3–4 minutes. Turn and sear the other side for about 2 minutes, then set the pan aside. The residual heat will continue to cook the mackerel very gently so that it is still moist and juicy when served.

To make the dressing, put the horseradish into a bowl, then add the remaining ingredients. Add a pinch of salt and pepper and whisk everything together.

To assemble the dish, divide the salad leaves between 6 plates, layer the mackerel, roast tomatoes, horseradish cream and pickled shallots on top, and there you have it – a mouth-wateringly beautiful lunchtime salad.

Tuna ceviche with spiralised cucumber

I have always been about a stone heavier than my ideal weight, although it's never really worried me – too many people in my life are too thin. But since turning forty, the half stone I usually put on during an intense run of filming just didn't drop off as it had in the past, so I ended up nearly three stone over what I wanted. This is foolish and selfish, and dangerous as well. Among the numerous reasons for not being overweight is that it is the number one risk factor for breast cancer, a disease that has caused havoc in my family.

Here we have one of the dishes I came up with on my diet, and it is so delicious that it's now a family favourite. Get one tuna steak per person from your fishmonger, or five in total if serving six, as below.

Serves 6

5 tuna steaks, as fresh as possible
4 cucumbers

FOR THE MARINADE
1 tsp English mustard powder
juice of 3 lemons

3 tbsp apple cider vinegar
1–2 small green chillies, deseeded to taste
2 large garlic cloves, peeled and grated
5cm piece of fresh root ginger, peeled and grated
sesame seeds

First make the marinade. In a bowl that will eventually fit the tuna as well, dissolve the mustard powder in the lemon juice and vinegar, then add the chillies, garlic and ginger. Stir together.

Cut the tuna into bite-sized rectangles and place in the bowl. Mix about so that the tuna turns pale as it is 'cooked' by the lemon juice. Transfer to the fridge for 1–3 hours.

Meanwhile, spiralise the cucumbers. If you don't have a spiraliser, use a potato peeler, cheese slicer or mandoline to cut the cucumbers into shavings. Divide between 6 plates.

Spoon the tuna and its marinade onto the cucumber, sprinkle over a few sesame seeds and serve immediately. It's that easy, and it's super-healthy and delicious.

Green bean salad

Scarily, we have been making *Location, Location, Location* for eighteen years, all that time travelling up and down the UK eating hotel breakfasts, pub lunches and room service suppers. Although there's been a huge improvement in what is available, there never seem to be enough greens on offer. Imagine my delight, then, when I came across a simple but delicious bean dish at Harts Hotel in Nottingham. It's now hugely popular in my house, though I have tweaked it quite a lot. You can easily tailor the amounts to serve any number of people.

Serves 6

350g green beans, trimmed
25g pine nuts
1 x 400g tin white beans, drained well
   (optional)
1–2 tbsp Gretchen's Salad Dressing (see
   page 60)

Parmesan, cheese shavings
3–4 basil sprigs
salt and freshly ground black pepper

Bring a large pan of water to the boil. Add the green beans, then cover and bring to the boil again. Turn the heat down to medium and simmer for 4–5 minutes, until the beans are cooked and tender – I pick one out towards the end and have a nibble to check they're cooked all the way through and not 'squeaky'.

While the beans are cooking, toast the pine nuts in a dry frying pan – there's no need to add any oil. Keep tossing them every now and then until they're golden.

Drain the green beans well in a colander and return them to the pan. Add the pine nuts, reserving a few to scatter over the top at the end, then the drained white beans (if using) and the salad dressing. Shave over a little Parmesan and roughly tear half the basil leaves over the top. Season and stir well so that the dressing coats everything in the pan. (You might want a bit more dressing if adding the white beans too.)

Spoon the mixture into a large bowl. Sprinkle with the remaining pine nuts, add a few more Parmesan shavings, and finish by tearing over the remaining basil leaves.

⸱ TIP ⸱

Sometimes I turn this side salad into more of a main course lunchtime feast by adding some smoked trout. Simply tear 2 fillets (around 125g) into flakes and fold them through at the last minute. Finish with a good squeeze of lemon juice and lots of black pepper too.

Tabbouleh

My first experience of Middle Eastern food was at Maroush in Beauchamp Place: their Jawaneh chicken wings are something else. When I did my history of art course at Christie's, I used to go to a nearby Lebanese kebab shop every day for my lunch. That was when I fell in love with tabbouleh, an affair that continues.

Many recipes for tabbouleh use a Middle Eastern spice mix, such as baharat (which can include allspice, black pepper, cardamom, cassia, cloves, coriander, cumin, nutmeg and chilli), or Lebanese seven-spice mix (paprika, pepper, cumin, cassia, cloves, coriander, cardamom and nutmeg), but you can mix your own. Simply use a pinch each of coriander, cinnamon, ginger, cloves and nutmeg, or any of the spices mentioned above, to make a teaspoonful of flavouring.

Serves 4

25g bulgur wheat
50 ml boiling water
300g ripe tomatoes
2 large bunches of flat-leaf parsley
small bunch of mint
6 spring onions
3 tbsp lemon juice
4 tbsp extra virgin olive oil

1 tsp mixed ground spices (see intoduction above)
salt and freshly ground black pepper

TO SERVE
at least 8 small Romaine or Little Gem lettuce leaves
4 ready-made flatbreads

Put the bulgur wheat in a small bowl and add the boiling water. Stir, then set aside for 20 minutes, or until the water has been absorbed. Drain in a sieve to be sure.

Meanwhile, use a sharp knife to remove the calyx and hard core from the tomatoes. (You can also skin the tomatoes and remove the seeds if you like, but I don't usually bother.) Quarter what's left, then cut into dice and put into a large serving bowl.

Pick the parsley and mint leaves, discarding the stalks or saving them for a stock. Chop the leaves finely, and do the same to the spring onions. Add them all to the tomatoes and mix well. When the bulgur wheat has absorbed all the water, use a fork to fluff it up and separate the grains. Add it to the tomatoes.

Drizzle the lemon juice and olive oil into the tomato mixture and season to taste with salt, pepper and your chosen spices. Mix well.

To serve, arrange the lettuce and flatbreads on 4 serving plates. Offer the tabbouleh in its bowl and ask people to help themselves, scooping tabbouleh into the leaves.

Salade niçoise

Hugh Fearnley-Whittingstall introduced me to this salad, which originates from Nice. I used to serve it years ago when I first started giving dinner parties, and I still make it now, although I have changed several things. For instance, you could add tomatoes, cucumber or sweet pepper, but these are not so authentic as the basic combination of tuna, potatoes, olives and green beans. You could leave the fish out altogether for a vegetarian version, or you could top the salad, as is very fashionable, with grilled fresh tuna instead of the tinned stuff. It's always a treat during the summer, either as a starter or a main course.

Serves 8

450g small new potatoes, scrubbed
8 large eggs
350g French beans, topped and tailed
450g tinned tuna in oil
3 soft lettuces, leaves separated
50g rocket leaves
75g small black olives
2 x 50g tins anchovy fillets in oil, drained
1–2 tbsp capers
handful of fresh basil leaves, torn
salt and freshly ground black pepper

FOR THE DRESSING
1 large garlic clove, peeled and crushed
3 tbsp extra virgin olive oil
3 tbsp sunflower oil (replace some of it with the tinned tuna oil if you wish)
3 tbsp white wine vinegar
2 tsp Dijon mustard
pinch of caster sugar

Put the potatoes in a large pan of boiling water and cook until tender, about 15–20 minutes. About 7 minutes before the potatoes are done, add the eggs to hardboil them; put the French beans in a steamer basket, cover with a lid and sit it above the potatoes. All three things should be ready at the same time.

Drain the potatoes and leave them to cool with the beans. Hold the eggs under cold water to stop them cooking any more, then peel off the shells. Cut them in half lengthways.

Drain the tuna and break it into small chunks. Keep the oil, which you can add to the dressing. Make the latter by mixing everything together in a lidded jar and shaking well. Alternatively, use a bowl and a whisk.

Arrange the lettuce and rocket leaves in a large salad bowl. Halve the potatoes and place on top with the beans. Trickle about half the dressing over these ingredients. Arrange the egg halves, tuna and anchovies artistically on top, then add the capers. Pour the rest of the dressing over the salad, but do not toss. Sprinkle with the torn basil leaves. Serve fairly swiftly, with lots of warm crusty bread and some wonderful French butter.

Roasted vegetables

To roast vegetables is simplicity itself, and they make a brilliant accompaniment to any manner of dish, from the Sunday roast to a simple chop supper. You can also eat them by themselves, with just a green salad and some crusty bread. They taste delicious, and the only work is the preparing and chopping – you must make sure that the pieces are all roughly the same size. Use any vegetables you like, but here I give you two ideas that are vaguely seasonal.

Ben likes to do roast vegetables, particularly in the summer. He is so casual about it, yet it never goes wrong ... except when he forgets while busy with the barbecue. Occasionally, days later, I have found a blackened tray of unidentifiable lumps in the Aga.

I consider this a non-recipe – just a template for you to use with whatever you have to hand, and in whatever quantities you want.

Serves 4–6

SUMMER
1 red pepper
1 yellow pepper
2 red onions
4 medium courgettes
1 aubergine
6 medium tomatoes
1 whole head of garlic
2 pinches of fresh thyme leaves
olive oil
salt and freshly ground black pepper

WINTER
4 carrots
4 parsnips
1 small butternut squash
200g small potatoes
1 small celeriac
1 whole head of garlic
2 pinches of fresh rosemary leaves
olive oil

Preheat the oven to 200°C/Fan 180°C/Gas 6.

Whether you're roasting veg in winter or summer, the method is the same. Peel, trim, deseed and chop the vegetables as appropriate, making sure they are all roughly the same size. Halve the head of garlic through the middle. Place everything in a suitably sized tray and season with salt and pepper. Sprinkle with the herbs and drizzle generously with olive oil.

Roast for anything from 30–45 minutes, or until the veg are tender. The timing will depend on how large the pieces are. Serve immediately, or eat them cold. If there are any leftovers, they can be used in a soup (see page 96).

Potato salad

This is the most basic of potato salads, and it can be multiplied very easily, making it perfect for barbecues or other summer parties. It's also easy to ring the changes by adding, for example, chopped hard-boiled egg (in which case, omit the optional extra yolk listed below), tiny shards of celery, crunchy bacon bits or chopped onion. You could try different herbs too, such as parsley, coriander or mint instead of chives, and throw in some fennel, poppy or celery seeds. If you fancy something a bit more exotic, add some curry powder, mango chutney or lime pickle. Ben makes this quite often, and uses his own mayonnaise, so it always tastes special.

Serves 4

500g new potatoes, scraped clean(ish)
1 tbsp olive oil
1 tbsp lemon juice
3 tbsp mayonnaise (homemade, or Hellmann's is fine)

3 tbsp plain yoghurt
1 medium egg yolk (optional)
2 tbsp chopped chives or spring onions
salt and freshly ground black pepper

Cook the potatoes in boiling salted water for 15–20 minutes, until tender. Drain and set aside to cool slightly. Cut into halves or quarters, then place in a serving bowl. Add the oil and lemon juice and mix gently but thoroughly. Leave until cold.

Meanwhile, combine the mayo and yoghurt in a small bowl, adding the egg yolk if you like a richer flavour and texture. Stir in salt and pepper to taste, then the chives or spring onions.

When the potatoes are cold, add the mayo mixture, stir well and serve.

⟩ TIP ⟨

Great-great-granny Minnie's recipe for mayonnaise is a gem, so here it is:
'Take a round-bottomed basin in which you have placed three yolks of eggs. Stir these briskly with a wooden spoon, adding a pinch of dry mustard and one of salt. When the mixture has stiffened into a paste take half a gill [70ml] of tarragon vinegar and a wine-glassful of the freshest oil and stir these in, a few drops at a time, pressing the paste against the side of the bowl. When all the oil has been worked into the sauce, drop by drop, then add two or three drops of water, which prevents the sauce from curdling.'

Sweet potato dauphinoise

I was recently given a copy of Sarah Raven's *Good Good Food,* and within the first hour I was cooking this recipe from it, but, in my usual fashion, adding a little more chilli, ginger and garlic. It's incredibly more-ish and would be perfect as a vegetarian main course, served simply with a salad, or as a side dish with meat, chicken or fish. It freezes well too.

Serves 4–6

1.5kg small to medium sweet potatoes
120g piece of fresh root ginger
1–2 red chillies, deseeded and chopped
4 garlic cloves, peeled
1 x 400ml tin coconut milk

grated zest and juice of 2 limes
2 heaped tbsp clear honey or maple syrup (optional)
salt and freshly ground black pepper

Preheat the oven to 180°C/Fan 160°C/Gas 4. (I cooked mine in the baking oven of my Aga.) Peel the sweet potatoes and slice them thinly. Place in a baking dish – there's no need to arrange them neatly.

Peel the ginger with the side of a teaspoon – this was a revelation, what a fantastic discovery! Put it straight in your blender, or chop it first if you think the blade might not cope with it. Add the chillies and garlic and blitz until finely chopped. Add the coconut milk, lime zest and juice, and the honey (if using). Blitz briefly to combine. Pour this liquid over the sweet potatoes and mix together with your hands. Season with salt and pepper, cover with a lid or foil and bake for an hour or so, until the potatoes are tender. Uncover and bake for another 15–20 minutes, until the top has browned a little.

⟩ TIP ⟨

On one occasion I thought I'd ruined this dauphinoise after adding more than double the required amount of ginger. My salvage operation was surprisingly successful, so here it is. I chopped and fried a red onion, added a large skinned and chopped tomato, some cumin and coriander seeds, a big spoonful of garlic purée, a fresh deseeded chilli and some garam masala. To this I added half the wrecked dauphinoise and some hot water. I let it simmer a little, then put it in a large lidded pot. I cut up the monkfish I had intended to fry for dinner, added it to the pot and whacked it in the oven for 15 minutes. Bingo! I had a sweet potato and monkfish curry. The next day I blitzed the rest of the wrecked dauphinoise in a blender with some cream cheese to make a spiced sweet potato sauce and served it with gnocchi. Desperation proved to be the mother of invention!

Trine's salsa verde

I think the first time I met Trine Miller, who was on the same art history course as me, was the night that one of my girlfriends dragged me into the Ladies at the Atlantic Bar in Piccadilly and took some tweezers to my eyebrows. Both experiences were life changing.

Trine's taste in all things is second to none, and her extraordinary calmness in the kitchen is a great reminder that stress and food should not come together. Once you make Trine's salsa verde, you will wonder how you ever entertained without it. It goes with lamb, fish, chicken, potatoes ... in fact, let me know if you find something it doesn't go with. Trine puts two or three generous bowls of it on the table so you can spoon as much as you want onto whatever you're eating.

Like Trine, who includes coriander just because she likes it, you can play with the herb combinations if you like. I sometimes add dill, rocket or even watercress, depending on what I am serving the salsa with.

Serves 4–6

1 bunch each of fresh flat-leaf parsley and coriander (add ½ bunch of mint if serving with lamb)
1 tinned anchovy (optional, but very nice with lamb)
1 tbsp capers

juice of ½ lemon if herb bunches are small, or a whole lemon if bunches are large
1 tsp Dijon mustard
good olive oil

If using a blender, whizz the leaves and everything else, apart from the oil.

If preparing by hand, chop the leaves on a board and place them a bowl. Add the lemon juice and mustard and stir to combine.

Pour in glugs of the oil and whizz or stir after each addition until you get the right consistency (you can always add more, so go easy at the beginning).

That's it! Transfer to a clean serving bowl.

My tomato salad dressing

Here is one of those things that once you do it, you can't believe you ever did it any other way. There are two versions, one with avocado, one without: it's prettier without the avocado, but not so creamy. This is more a method than a recipe, and you can chuck in anything you fancy: garlic, basil, coriander, feta cheese, mustard, honey, lemon juice, red wine vinegar... (Ben calls sweetening salad dressing with honey or sugar 'Sloane food', a low blow.) Just don't keep your tomatoes in the fridge.

- Take the tomatoes you would have put in your salad and cut them into halves or quarters, depending on size. Put them into a smallish plastic storage container (I swear by the ones from Joseph Joseph because they colour-code the lids, which means you don't spend hours trying to match tops and bottoms). Add salt and pepper, 1 tablespoon olive oil and 1 teaspoon apple cider vinegar (but this can be any oil/vinegar combo, depending on your favourites).

- Put the lid on the container and shake so that the tomatoes give up their juice to make the salad dressing. You can then tip both the tomatoes and their juices over your salad at the last moment in place of a more conventional dressing.

- Tomatoes tossed in lemon juice rather than vinegar are more colourful, and look great with broccoli, spinach or peas. (I am not shy about chucking cooked and raw vegetables together.)

- If you add chopped avocado to the container along with the tomatoes, you get a creamier sauce, but it is a bit sludge-coloured.

Gretchen's salad dressing

My mother-in-law Gretchen was born in South Africa, to an Afrikaans father (of Bavarian missionary stock) and a mother whose maternal ancestors came from Devon. Before she married, Gretchen lived for a while with friends in France, then came to Britain, where she has stayed. Much of her time here, apart from raising family, has been spent keeping shop at The Lacquer Chest in Kensington Church Street. She also has a home in Italy, near her sister. This is a very roundabout way of saying that I don't know whether this dressing is French or Italian, or from further afield, but it is brilliant. I like it with crudités, green salad, tomatoes and basil, or on cold beetroot. It's a winner if you go anywhere to stay: simply say, 'Can I make some dressing?' and you are a dream guest.

Makes 400ml

300ml olive oil
100ml white wine vinegar
3 tsp Colman's English mustard paste
1 small garlic clove, peeled and crushed
salt and freshly ground black or white pepper

Put all the ingredients, except the salt and pepper, into a small container – Gretchen uses a clean, lidded mustard pot – and shake until everything emulsifies.

If you are away from home and don't have a small pot, you can make the dressing in the bottom of a salad bowl, stirring it together with a fork. The quantities can be adjusted to serve any number, the most important proportions being three parts oil to one part vinegar.

Season the dressing just before you use it.

The dressing will keep well for up to a week, so it is worth making quite a lot at a time, especially in the summer when we eat so many salads.

Chapter 3

Big Dishes

Most of the dishes I cook are 'big' dishes, as we are a family of six – my partner Ben and myself, my stepsons, Hal and Orion, and our sons, Bay and Oscar. Ben and I also entertain a lot, both in London and at Grange, our house in Devon. We know three or four couples who each have three or four children, so you only need to have two conversations on the phone and suddenly you are feeding well in excess of twelve people. This happens a lot, so big dishes are de rigueur. As a result, I tend to rely on recipes that can be prepared in advance, doubled or trebled easily, frozen, or that don't need much last-minute attention. When people are coming to eat, or to stay at Grange for the weekend, I don't want to be faffing around in the kitchen: I want to be chatting and making them cocktails.

As you'll see, most of the dishes in this chapter are stewy, long cooked and easy to serve. They are the easiest things when catering for large numbers, as well as the easiest to expand in some way when people who said they weren't coming change their mind, and you suddenly have to cater for sixteen rather than twelve. It can be a case of 'family hold back', but in reality you can be a little meaner on the meat front, and up the starch quantities, making more rice or couscous, or baking more potatoes. (The get-ahead hints to do with vegetables on page 225 will also help in instances like this.) With a huge bowl of green salad and another big bean or tomato salad, it will all look very generous and colourful.

I cook most of these big dishes in Devon, where I have more time for cooking and entertaining. Sometimes I even bring food back to London, like the time I transported a lamb tagine for a class party at the boys' school. I have a large collection of giant food containers, bought mostly in Kenya, where travelling around with vast amounts of food is quite normal.

I have to admit that for many years my cooking was very hit and miss and I just went by instinct. It was only when filming *Kirstie's Handmade Britain*, which involved working with a number of talented chefs, that I was able to combine my instinct with a more solid foundation of knowledge and experience. Now I turn to my recipe books almost every day, and I cook from other people's recipes all the time – there are a few of them in this book – but I still tweak and adjust as I go along, often because I don't have all the ingredients listed. This is no bad thing, as it's important to trust your instinct as a cook.

As my confidence has grown, my happiest time of the week is now between 10 and 11.15 on a Sunday morning. I am in the kitchen down in Devon, the Archers' omnibus is on the radio and I am cooking something for lunch. There is no rush, no stress, as no one is going to pitch up until at least one o'clock. It's my new pleasure – chopping, sizzling, listening to the radio, knowing that people we like are coming to eat and drink. That is just bliss.

Grange lamb & apricot tagine

We have loads of great mutton in Devon, so I often make this wonderful recipe by Hugh Fearnley-Whittingstall. I have adapted it to include more chilli, garlic and ginger, tossed in some chickpeas – perfect for when you need to bulk up the dish to serve more – and a bag of my beloved spinach. The result is wildly edible and freezes brilliantly. It's great with couscous, rice or roast potatoes (see page 225).

Serves 4–6

1kg shoulder of lamb, boned and cut into 3cm chunks (about 840g boned meat)
1 cinnamon stick
2 tsp ground cumin
1 tsp each of sweet paprika, hot paprika, ground coriander and ground turmeric
4 cardamom pods, lightly crushed
½–1 tsp dried chilli flakes
2 fresh red chillies, chopped
1 x 400g tin chopped tomatoes
2 onions, peeled and finely sliced
40g fresh root ginger, peeled and grated
1 tsp saffron strands
1 tbsp tomato purée
2 tbsp olive oil

6 garlic cloves, peeled and finely chopped
250g dried apricots
2 tbsp clear honey
a little pared zest and the juice of 1 lemon
1 x 400g tin chickpeas, drained and rinsed
1 x 200g bag baby leaf spinach
salt and freshly ground black pepper

TO FINISH AND GARNISH
handful of coriander leaves, finely chopped, plus a few sprigs
small handful of mint leaves, finely chopped
lemon wedges

Put the lamb into a bowl, add all the dry spices and the fresh chillies and mix well. Cover and leave to stand in a cool place for at least 3 hours.

Put the spiced lamb, tomatoes and onions into a large pan and add just enough water to cover. Bring to a simmer, then add the ginger, saffron, tomato purée, olive oil and garlic. Stir well and bring back to a simmer. Lower the heat and cook very gently, with the lid partially on, for 2 hours.

Add the apricots, honey, lemon zest and juice. Cook gently for another 30 minutes, adding a little water if you think it is needed. About 10 minutes before the end of this time, add the chickpeas and spinach, and allow them to warm through. Taste and adjust the seasoning.

Stir in the chopped coriander and mint. Serve the lamb, garnished with coriander sprigs and with lemon wedges on the side. Accompany with Moroccan breads, boiled rice or couscous finished with a little butter.

Chicken pie

My mother-in-law's shop – The Lacquer Chest in Kensington Church Street – is not far away from Sally Clarke's restaurant and deli. When I first came to London, I lived in Peel Street, and Sally's deli was where I went for coffee and croissants. Homemade bread was on offer, a small counter with artisan cheeses, and a larger one with biscuits, quiches, her very decadent chocolate truffles, plus wines, seasonal vegetables and all sorts. Gretchen is a careful spender, but will happily go into Clarke's and blow a fortune!

Another of Sally's offerings is chicken pie. You can buy this in slices, or the whole thing, and it is absolutely delicious. She hasn't published a recipe, but I have experimented and made something that doesn't look nearly so professional as hers, but tastes almost as good.

Serves 8–10

25g butter
1 tbsp olive oil
2 leeks (about 300g in total), sliced
200g chestnut mushrooms, finely sliced
small handful (about 10g) freshly
    chopped parsley
100ml double cream
1 tbsp water
200g cooked chicken (you'll need 2 raw
    chicken breasts if you're roasting them
    from scratch, see tip overleaf)
salt and freshly ground black pepper

FOR THE PASTRY
220g plain flour, plus a little extra for
    dusting
110g unsalted butter, chopped
good pinch of salt
1–2 tbsp water
1 large egg, beaten

First make the pastry. Put the flour, butter and salt into the bowl of a food processor and whizz until the mixture looks like breadcrumbs.

Add the water and whizz again until the mixture starts to form clumps. Tip into a bowl and gently bring it together with your hands. Knead very lightly until smooth. Divide into two pieces, roughly two-thirds and one-third, and shape each into a disc. Wrap in greaseproof paper or clingfilm and chill for 20 minutes.

Roll out the larger piece of pastry on a lightly floured board and use to line a tart tin 20–21cm wide and 2cm deep. Prick the base all over and return to the fridge for 15 minutes.

CONTINUED OVERLEAF ❯

Preheat the oven to 190°C/Fan 170°C/Gas 5 and slide a baking sheet inside to heat up.

Line the pastry case with baking parchment and fill with baking beans. Bake for 15 minutes, then remove the paper and beans and continue to bake until the pastry looks dry, a few minutes longer. Brush some beaten egg over the base (not the sides), reserving the remaining egg for later. Return the pastry case to the oven for 3–4 minutes to dry out. Set the tin aside and turn the oven off.

Now make the filling. Heat the butter and oil in a pan, add the leeks and cook gently over a low heat, covered with the lid, for 10 minutes. Season well. Add the mushrooms, increase the heat slightly, and continue to cook for 8–10 minutes, until they are golden. Season well. Stir in the parsley, cream and water and cook for 1–2 minutes. Spoon into a bowl and set aside to cool.

Tear the cooked chicken into large chunks and stir through the cooled leek mixture. Taste for seasoning, then spoon into the baked pastry case.

Preheat the oven to 190°C/Fan 170°C/Gas 5.

Roll out the remaining pastry on a lightly floured board and use to cover the filling. Trim the edges, sealing them all around. Make two holes in the top for steam to escape.

Brush the surface with the remaining beaten egg, sprinkle with salt and bake in the oven for 40 minutes, until golden.

⸙ TIP ⸙

If you need to roast the chicken first, put the meat in a roasting tin, drizzle with a little oil and season with salt and black pepper. Roast in an oven preheated to 200°C/Fan 180°C/Gas 6 for around 20 minutes. To check it's cooked, slice through the middle – there should be no signs of pink juices or pink flesh. If there are, cook for another 5 minutes or so, until it's cooked right through.

Jane's cottage pie

I spent my late teens doing a variety of jobs and living at home in London. Following a row with my mum about a bounced cheque, I lived for a while with an artist friend of mine called Jane, who is passionate about food, and doesn't believe in anything being ordinary. This is her exotic version of cottage pie, which includes mushroom ketchup and advieh, a Persian spice mix that can include saffron, cinnamon, rosebuds, sesame, coriander and cardamom. Although it is not traditional, I am very fond of this dish because of its flavours, and also because it may well have been the first complete dish I ever learnt to make.

Serves 8

1.4kg floury potatoes, peeled
freshly grated nutmeg
100g butter
salt and freshly ground black pepper

FOR THE MEAT FILLING
50g butter
2 onions, peeled and chopped

2 carrots, peeled and sliced
200g mushrooms, finely sliced
sunflower oil
1.2kg best-quality beef mince
1 tsp advieh
1 tbsp mushroom ketchup
1 tbsp Worcestershire sauce
450–500ml hot beef stock

Cut the potatoes into chunks and cook in boiling salted water until tender, about 20 minutes. Drain, season with salt, pepper and nutmeg, and add most of the butter. Mash by hand, keeping the potatoes quite rugged – you don't want them too smooth. Cover and set aside while you cook the meat filling.

Melt the butter in a large pan, then add the onions and carrots. Cook gently until starting to soften, about 5–8 minutes. Add the mushrooms and cook until starting to soften and turn golden, about 2–3 minutes. Season to taste with salt and pepper. Transfer this mixture to a plate and set aside.

Return the pan to a medium heat, add a little oil, then about a third of the mince, flattening it with the back of a spoon so it browns evenly. Turn and continue to cook until golden. Add to the plate with the onion mixture and cook the remaining mince in two batches in the same way. Return the onion and meat mixture to the pan, add the remaining filling ingredients and 450ml of the stock. Simmer for about 25 minutes. If it gets too dry, add the extra 50ml stock. Taste for seasoning.

Preheat the oven to 180°C/Fan 160°C/Gas 4. Tip the meat mixture into a large baking dish and spoon the potato on top, forking it into peaks. Dot with the remaining butter and bake for 40–45 minutes, until the top is nicely browned.

Jools' fish pie

When I was young, free and single, there was a fish restaurant in Westbourne Grove called Zucca, and the co-owner, Jamie Sherriff, once cooked me a fish pie with spinach. I thought the combination was just wonderful. I didn't get the Zucca recipe, but this version from Jools Oliver comes close to that long-ago favourite. Try, as Jools recommends, to get the fish from sustainable sources.

Serves 8

1.5kg floury potatoes, peeled
4 large free-range eggs (optional)
300g skinless, boneless white fish, such as coley, whiting, haddock, cod, from sustainable sources
200g skinless boneless salmon from sustainable sources
200g skinless, boneless undyed smoked haddock, from sustainable sources
200g baby spinach
extra virgin olive oil
1 whole nutmeg

FOR THE SAUCE
50g unsalted butter
50g plain flour
2 fresh bay leaves
350ml quality fish stock
350ml semi-skimmed milk
1 heaped tsp English mustard
50g Cheddar cheese
juice of ½ lemon
a few sprigs of fresh flat-leaf parsley (optional)
freshly ground black pepper

Preheat the oven to 200°C/Fan 180°C/Gas 6. Cut the potatoes into 2cm chunks and boil for 15 minutes, or until tender. Add the eggs (if using) for the last 8 minutes.

Meanwhile, make the sauce. Melt the butter in a heavy-bottomed pan over a low heat and stir in the flour. Add the bay, then bit by bit, add the stock and the milk, stirring after every addition until you have a smooth, silky sauce. Bring to the boil, then reduce to a simmer and cook for 10 minutes, or until thickened. Stir in the mustard, grate in half the cheese, then squeeze in the lemon juice. Pick, finely chop and stir in the parsley (if using), then keep stirring until the cheese is melted. Season with a little black pepper, then remove from the heat.

Get yourself a 25 x 30cm baking dish. Check that there aren't any stray bones lurking in the fish fillets, then slice into 2.5cm chunks and spread them evenly over the base of the dish. Wilt and add the spinach, then peel, quarter and add the eggs (if using). Remove the bay leaves from the white sauce, pour it over the dish and allow to cool slightly. Drain the potatoes well and mash with a little olive oil, a splash of milk and a few scrapings of nutmeg. Spoon the potatoes over the pie and scuff up the surface with a fork. Grate the remaining Cheddar over the top and bake in the oven for 45 minutes, or until the fish is cooked through and the top is golden.

Mdoroni Swahili fish curry

Having spent quite a lot of time in India and East Africa, I have enjoyed some very special spicy dishes. This recipe is one of my favourites, and it comes from Naomi, who is the cook at Mdoroni, a beautiful house in Kilifi on the Kenyan coast. Kenya is a fantastic country, which I first visited when I was twenty-five. This delicious fish curry brings back happy memories of that amazing trip.

Serves 4–6

500g white fish fillets, cubed, or peeled
    prawns
2 tbsp plain yoghurt (optional)
handful of fresh coriander leaves

FOR THE CURRY SAUCE
4 tbsp coconut or sunflower oil
2 large onions, peeled and finely chopped
2 chillies of your choice, chopped
480ml water
4 garlic cloves, peeled and crushed to
    a paste

small knob of fresh root ginger, peeled
    and grated
½ tsp ground turmeric
1 tsp cumin seeds, freshly ground
2 tbsp medium curry powder
½ tsp tomato purée
2 medium tomatoes, roughly chopped
1 large sweet green pepper, seeded and
    roughly chopped
1 bunch of fresh coriander, leaves and stalks
1 chicken stock cube
1 x 250ml carton coconut cream
salt and freshly ground black pepper

First start the sauce: put the oil in a medium saucepan over a medium heat. When hot, add the onions and stir them for 2 minutes, until nearly brown. Add the chillies and fry until the onions are dark brown. Turn the heat down to low.

Holding the saucepan lid in one hand, add 50ml of the water to the onion mix, then immediately replace the lid and cook for 1 minute. Turn the heat up to high and stir until the water dissolves in the oil.

Add the garlic and ginger and fry for 3 minutes, then add the turmeric, cumin and curry powder. Fry for about 4–5 minutes, until the spices smell good. Stir in the tomato purée as they cook.

Put the tomatoes, green pepper and fresh coriander (leaves and stalks) into a food processor. Add 2 tablespoons of the remaining water and blend to a smooth paste. Add this to the hot spice mixture, and keep cooking and stirring over a moderate heat until it becomes a smooth purée and smells beautifully aromatic.

CONTINUED OVERLEAF ❯

Crumble in the stock cube and add salt and pepper to taste. (Be careful as the stock cube will probably be quite salty already.) Now pour in the remaining 400ml water and leave the mixture to simmer and bubble for 5 minutes. Add the coconut cream and bubble for another 5 minutes.

Gently tip in the fish cubes or prawns and cook for 4–8 minutes (the time depends on how big the pieces are and how high the heat is). If using white fish, do not stir as it will break up: simply shake the pan if necessary to mix the fish into the sauce.

When the fish turns opaque and is cooked all the way through, turn the heat off and add the yoghurt (if using) and the fresh coriander leaves. Shake the saucepan to spread them through the curry. Leave to stand for 2 minutes, then serve with chapattis or poppadoms, rice, cucumber raita (topped with a few toasted cumin seeds and a little extra chopped cucumber) and mango chutney.

Naomi says 'Enjoy'.

Slow-cooked Asian lamb

Although we have an Aga and could do this recipe in the slow or simmering oven, I like the result you get from using a crockpot or slow-cooker. The texture of the lamb is just like that of pulled pork (and of course you could do a joint of pork in exactly the same way). I have suggested adding some star anise, as this deepens the spiciness, but it's up to you.

Serves 4–6

1 x 1.8kg shoulder of lamb, on the bone,
   or 1 x 2kg leg of lamb
2 tbsp vegetable oil
1 x 7.5cm piece of fresh root ginger,
   peeled and grated
4 large garlic cloves, peeled and crushed
   or grated
2 fresh red chillies, finely chopped

4 tbsp soy sauce
1 tbsp Worcestershire sauce
2 tbsp clear honey or maple syrup
1 large onion, peeled and halved
1 lemon, halved
3 star anise (optional)
500ml light chicken or vegetable stock
   (a stock cube is fine)

If using a slow-cooker, make sure your joint of lamb will fit in it. If using a conventional oven, preheat it to 170°C/Fan 150°C/Gas 3.

Heat the oil in a large frying pan and brown the lamb on all sides. Place in the slow-cooker or a roasting pan. (If using an Aga, brown the lamb in the roasting oven for about 20 minutes, then do the rest in the simmering oven.)

Mix the ginger, garlic, chillies, soy sauce, Worcester sauce and honey in a bowl. Smear all over the lamb. Tuck the onion halves, lemon halves and star anise (if using) around the joint, then pour the stock around it – you don't want to disturb that sticky topping.

Set the slow-cooker to low, put the lid on and leave the lamb to cook for around 6–7 hours. In the Aga, or a conventional oven preheated as above, it will take about 2½–3 hours (the longer the better, to be honest). Keep an eye on it throughout the cooking time, and add a little more water or stock if it looks too dry. You want to have a liquid sauce at the end. Test by using a fork to pull a little bit of meat from the joint. If it comes away very easily, it's done. If not, continue to cook in the oven until it does. When ready, the meat will be very tender, actually falling off the bone, so be careful when moving it from pot to plate.

We serve these tender strands of meat with their juices, some quick stir-fried greens and rice or noodles.

Kofta, apricot and prune biryani

One of the best things about doing an annual Christmas show is learning new recipes for food and cocktails from a selection of brilliant professionals. High on my list of favourites is Angela Malik, who is such a kind and encouraging teacher. I hope my passion for all things Indian comes through loud and clear in this book, but learning this recipe from Angela really changed my cooking because there is nothing you cannot cook in her masala sauce. Ben brings all sorts of stuff home – rabbit, pheasant, mutton and various kinds of fish – and all have been chucked in the masala and come out the better for it

Biryani is an all-in-one rice dish containing meat and veg. Angela's version, with lamb koftas, dried fruit and masala sauce, is superb. I particularly like the crusty bits of rice at the bottom of the pan.

Serves 8

500g leg of lamb meat, minced, or use 500g
    lamb mince
1 onion, peeled and grated
1 large egg, beaten
2 tsp ginger paste
1 tsp garlic paste
2 tsp garam masala
½ fresh green chilli, chopped
2 tsp chopped coriander leaves
salt, to taste
1 tbsp sunflower oil

FOR THE MASALA SAUCE
3 tbsp sunflower oil
2 medium onions, peeled and finely
    chopped or whizzed in a blender
2 tbsp ginger paste
1 tbsp garlic paste
1 cinnamon stick
1 bay leaf
1 black or green cardamom pod
200g chopped tomatoes (tinned or fresh)
100ml water
1 tsp ground cumin
1 tsp ground coriander

1 tsp garam masala
½ tsp ground turmeric
¼ tsp red chilli powder
1 tsp salt
3 tbsp plain yoghurt

FOR LAYERING THE BIRYANI
3 oranges, zest of 2 and juice of all
100g pitted prunes
100g dried apricots
2 onions, peeled and sliced
1 tbsp sunflower oil, for frying
50g butter

FOR THE RICE
450g basmati rice
3 litres water
2 tsp salt
2 black or green cardamom pods
2 x 5cm cinnamon sticks
4 cloves
2 bay leaves
bunch of fresh coriander, stalks chopped
    and leaves roughly chopped

CONTINUED OVERLEAF ❯

Start by soaking the fruit for layering the biryani and preparing the rice. Put half the orange zest into a bowl, then add all the orange juice and the dried fruit. Set aside. Wash the rice in a sieve, tip into a large bowl and cover with cold water. Set aside.

Now prepare the masala sauce. Heat the oil in a heavy-based saucepan. Add the onions and fry over a moderate heat, stirring occasionally, until golden brown. This will take at least 10 minutes. Add the ginger, garlic and whole spices. Fry for about a minute, until you feel the ginger paste starting to stick to the pan. Add the tomatoes and water. Cover and cook on a medium heat, mashing the mixture down every now and then, until it becomes a pulp, about 10 minutes. Add the ground spices, salt and yoghurt and stir thoroughly.

To make the koftas, put the lamb into a bowl and add the onion, egg, flavourings, coriander and salt. Mix well and taste for seasoning. Shape the mince mixture into balls about 3–5cm in diameter. Heat the oil in a large frying pan. When hot, fry the koftas, in batches, on all sides for 2–3 minutes. Set aside on a plate.

While the koftas are cooking, fry the 'layering' onion in the oil in a saucepan until golden, at least 10 minutes. Stir frequently, then set aside once done.

Drain the rice. Boil the 3 litres of water in a large saucepan with the salt. Add the dried spices, bay leaves and some of the chopped coriander leaves to the pan. Once it reaches a rolling boil, add the rice. Bring back to the boil and cook for about 4 minutes: it should still be hard in the middle. Drain the rice and remove the cinnamon and bay, then add extra salt to taste. Mix in the orange zest reserved from the layering ingredients. Decant the rice into a large bowl.

Preheat the oven to 170°C/Fan 150°C/Gas 3. Drain the fruit, reserving the liquid.

Now you have to layer the biryani. In a large, wide ovenproof casserole pan, melt the butter. Add half the rice mixture and spread evenly in the bottom of the pan. Add a layer of half the fried onions, then half the apricots and prunes. Add all the koftas in one layer, then cover with the masala sauce. Spoon the remaining rice on top and spread it over the koftas. Top with the remaining fruit, and finish with the rest of the fried onions.

Pour the reserved orange juice all over the layers. Cover the pan tightly with a lid and cook on a high heat for 5 minutes. Transfer to the oven for a further 30–40 minutes. After 30 minutes, pinch a few rice grains between your fingers. If they are tender, take the dish out of the oven. If overcooked, the rice will turn mushy.

The biryani can be served straight from the pan, or turned onto a large, flat dish, in both cases garnished with the remaining coriander. The crusty layer from the bottom of the pan is a delicacy and should be served around the edges of the dish.

Pomegranate raita

This is what Angela Malik would serve with her wonderful biryani (see page 82) – such an interesting change from the usual cucumber raita, and quite good enough to eat by itself.

Serves 4

1 pomegranate
400ml plain yoghurt
handful of chopped fresh coriander, leaves and stalks, plus a few whole leaves to garnish
½–¾ tsp roasted cumin powder (i.e. cumin seeds dry-roasted and ground)
good pinch of red chilli powder
salt and freshly ground black pepper

Lightly press down on the pomegranate as you roll it around with your hand on a hard surface (applying a little pressure helps to loosen the seeds). Slice the pomegranate in half, hold one half over a bowl and tap the outside of the fruit with a wooden spoon – the seeds should tumble out. There might be too many for the raita, so munch away.

Mix together the yoghurt, most of the pomegranate seeds and the coriander. Season to taste with salt, lots of black pepper, the cumin and red chilli powder. Garnish with the remaining pomegranate seeds and a few coriander leaves.

Lasagne

I love lasagne, but Ben hates it, so much so that I am rarely allowed to serve it. Up to the age of sixteen, he lived in London and Italy, and had wonderful food cooked by his mother, Gretchen. He probably liked lasagne then, but then he left home and moved in with a girlfriend in the Fulham Road. This was the time when the first ready-meals were being sold, and lasagne was probably one of them. Fulham Sloanes were quite keen on ready-meals, which might explain Ben's present-day aversion to the dish.

Lasagne is fiddly to make, but it can be prepared in advance and, best of all, can be frozen. It's great for a crowd – the quantities can easily be doubled or trebled – and the kids love it too.

Serves 6–8

250g lasagne sheets (the ones you don't need to pre-cook are the easiest)
100g Parmesan or pecorino cheese, freshly grated
100g mozzarella cheese (optional)

FOR THE MINCED BEEF SAUCE
2 tbsp olive oil
1 large onion, peeled and chopped
3 garlic cloves, peeled and chopped
130g bacon or pancetta pieces
1kg minced beef
2 tbsp tomato purée

a sprinkling of dried oregano
2 x 400g tins chopped tomatoes
150ml inexpensive red wine
1 beef stock cube, dissolved in 100ml boiling water
salt and freshly ground black pepper

FOR THE BÉCHAMEL SAUCE
1 litre milk
1 bay leaf
50g butter
50g plain flour
freshly grated nutmeg

To start the beef sauce, heat the olive oil in a large pan and add the onion and garlic. Cook gently for about 10 minutes, until soft. Add the bacon and mince and stir well to break up the clumps. After about 5 minutes, when the mince has turned from grey to brown, add salt and pepper, the tomato purée, oregano, chopped tomatoes, wine and stock. Stir everything together and leave to bubble, uncovered, for about 40 minutes. It should be thick and not too liquid.

Meanwhile, heat the milk for the béchamel in a pan until almost boiling. Take off the heat, add the bay leaf and leave to infuse for about 20 minutes.

CONTINUED OVERLEAF ❯

Melt the butter in a clean medium pan over a low heat. Slowly sprinkle in the flour, stirring all the time. Once you have a smooth paste that's beginning to bubble, start adding the milk slowly, stirring continuously. Keep stirring until the sauce is smooth and has thickened slightly. Discard the bay leaf, then season with salt, pepper and nutmeg.

Preheat the oven to 190°C/Fan 170°C/Gas 5. Set out a baking dish measuring about 30 x 22 x 7cm.

To assemble the lasagne, spread about a quarter of the mince in the bottom of your chosen dish. Cover with some of the pasta sheets, overlapping them slightly if necessary. Spread some of the béchamel over them and add a sprinkling of the Parmesan. Repeat these layers (you might not need all the pasta), finishing with béchamel and Parmesan on top.

If you like, slice the mozzarella and use as another layer, or simply grate it over the top before baking.

Bake for about 40 minutes, or until the pasta is cooked and the top is golden. (A lasagne made in a bigger dish will take a little longer to cook.) All you need as accompaniment is a huge bowl of green salad.

Havyarli spaghetti

I first went to Turkey when I was 18, and I have been going back ever since. It's a place I adore. Turkish food is wonderful, reflecting the country's extraordinary historic and geographic importance. I am a huge fan of Jason Goodwin's *Yashim* books, which cleverly combine 19th-century Constantinople murder mysteries with food. My greatest friend in Turkey is a great foodie: he gets it from his mother, who is a wonderful cook and this recipe is hers. When I said I wanted to include it in this book, she was mortified and said, 'It's from the old days, when caviar was much cheaper in Turkey.' But the whole concept – the mixture of salty fish flavours, cheese and pasta – is delicious.

I usually replace the caviar with codfish roe or something like that, which is a fraction of the price. You could also try orange keta (salmon), black lumpfish roe, or some bottarga (the dried roe of tuna or grey mullet). Bottarga is produced in Dalyan in Turkey, so that would be quite authentic in this recipe. Cut it into wafer-thin slices, or grate on top of the spaghetti.

Serves 6

500g spaghetti or angel hair pasta

FOR THE SAUCE
600ml double cream
2 tbsp olive oil
200g ricotta cheese
juice of ¼ lemon

grated zest of 1 lemon
salt and freshly ground black pepper

FOR THE TOPPING
caviar, as much as you can afford,
    or a cheaper alternative (see above)

Cook the pasta in boiling salted water until al dente. (This should take about 10 minutes for spaghetti, 5 minutes for the angel hair, but follow the packet instructions for best results.)

Meanwhile, make the sauce: place the double cream and olive oil in a saucepan over a medium heat and bring to a simmer. Add the ricotta and allow it to melt; this takes only a minute or two. Remove from the heat and add the lemon juice and zest, plus salt and pepper to taste. Mix well.

Thoroughly warm a large serving bowl. (I buy those Victorian washing bowl and jug sets, which are very cheap, and use the bowl for huge salads or dishes like this.) When the pasta is ready, drain it, then put straight into the pan of hot sauce and mix well. Tip into the warmed bowl and take immediately to the table. Your guests can help themselves to pasta, adding a modicum of caviar on top.

Winter vegetable soup

My great-great granny, Lady Hindlip, made a lovely vegetable soup a bit like minestrone: 'Cut up three or four potatoes, add a proportionate quantity of beans (dried ones are best), onions, carrots and celery (sliced), and if in season, sliced vegetable marrow and pumpkin-rind. Boil all these in a quarter of a saucepan of water till the potatoes are quite soft, adding, of course, salt. Then add a quarter of a pound of rice or macaroni. Boil a little longer, as the rice ought not to be soft, and before taking off the fire add an ounce of butter or the orthodox spoonful of fine olive oil and as much Parmesan cheese. Stir a few minutes and serve.'

Below we have a cockle-warming soup with lots of texture and flavour, also a bit like minestrone, but without the pasta. It is perfect for a winter's day lunch.

Serves 6–8

2 tbsp extra virgin olive oil
1 large onion, peeled and finely chopped
2 celery sticks, roughly chopped
2 medium carrots or parsnips, peeled and roughly chopped
2 garlic cloves, peeled and crushed
2 pinches of chilli flakes
1 x 6cm piece of fresh root ginger, peeled and grated
1.2 litres chicken stock, preferably homemade
1 tbsp tomato purée

½ small butternut squash, peeled and cut into cubes
1 large potato (about 250g), peeled and cut into cubes
¼ Savoy cabbage, cut into thin ribbons
1 x 400g tin chickpeas, drained and rinsed
handful of fresh herb leaves, e.g. parsley and basil, to serve, roughly chopped at the last minute
salt and freshly ground black pepper

Heat the oil in a large saucepan over a medium-high heat. Add the onion, celery and carrots or parsnips, and cook over a lowish heat, stirring occasionally, for about 10 minutes, until the vegetables are starting to turn golden at the edges. Add the garlic, chilli flakes, ginger and some salt, and give everything a really good stir. Allow to cook gently until you start to smell the lovely aroma of the garlic.

Add the stock and tomato purée, cover with a lid and bring to the boil. Add the squash and potato, cover again and bring back to the boil. Reduce the heat and simmer, partially covered, until the vegetables are tender, about 15 minutes.

Stir in the cabbage and chickpeas and return to the boil. Simmer for 3–4 minutes, until the cabbage is tender and the chickpeas are warm. Roughly chop the herbs, stir them into the soup and season to taste. Serve immediately with crusty bread.

Leftovers soup

I eat soup all the time, yet I rarely use a recipe because for me soup is leftovers, and leftovers are soup (although I must admit I do keep some leftovers to be fried up with rice – see page 99). The idea of using fresh ingredients for soup seems very extravagant, but that's not to say I never do it.

The basis of this soup is chicken stock (I always try to have plenty in the freezer, made from carcasses or bones that I freeze in bags until there are enough to make a batch). Almost any vegetables can be added, but go easy on potato, as that would make the soup too starchy. A strong veg base is the best, which is why I add my favourite – raw spinach. This produces a soup of the most vivid green.

Serves 4–6

2 tbsp olive oil
1 onion, peeled and finely chopped
2 celery sticks, finely chopped
4 garlic cloves, peeled and crushed
25g fresh root ginger, peeled and
  chopped
1 fresh red chilli, chopped

300g cooked vegetables (I used
  courgettes, peas and potato), chopped
  into bite-sized chunks
150g fresh spinach, well washed, thick
  stalks removed
1 bay leaf
1 litre stock, preferably homemade
salt and freshly ground black pepper

Heat the oil in a large saucepan over a medium heat and add the onion and celery. Fry for about 7 minutes, then add the garlic, ginger and chilli – my favourite flavouring trinity – and fry gently for 1–2 minutes, just until the garlic starts to turn golden; you don't want it to burn.

Add the cooked vegetables, spinach, bay leaf and stock. Bring to the boil, then simmer for 20 minutes or so, until everything is well heated through.

Remove the bay leaf, then blend the soup in the pan using a stick blender, or blitz in a food processor. I like a smooth soup, but you can leave it a little chunky if you prefer. I enjoy this particular soup cold, which is delicious.

⊱ TIP ⊰

Another great way of making a tasty but dull-looking soup appear more appetising is to add beetroot. I love its flavour, but long before you get to the flavour you get the glorious colour, and then your delicious brown sludge looks as good as it tastes.

Coronation chicken

I adore this recipe, the most delicious, versatile dish ever invented by a person's great-great-grandmother. Yes, it is thought that my great-great-granny, Minnie, Lady Hindlip, came up with the recipe that inspired Coronation Chicken, recreated in 1953 by Rosemary Hume of the Cordon Bleu Cookery School. This particular version comes courtesy of Felicity Cloake, who includes it in her book *Perfect Too*, and I often serve it at summer parties or picnics.

Serves 6

1 chicken, about 1.5kg
1 cinnamon stick
5 black peppercorns
pinch of saffron strands
1 tsp salt
1 bay leaf
2cm knob of fresh root ginger, kept whole

2 tbsp good curry powder
2cm piece of fresh root ginger, peeled
  and finely chopped
2 tsp Worcestershire sauce
200ml homemade mayonnaise
200ml Greek yoghurt
salt and freshly ground black pepper

FOR THE CURRY SAUCE
5 tbsp good-quality mango chutney
50g ready-to-eat dried apricots, finely
  chopped

TO FINISH
small bunch of fresh coriander, chopped,
  plus a few sprigs
50g flaked almonds, toasted

Put the chicken, breast-side up, in a large pan or ovenproof casserole dish, along with the cinnamon, peppercorns, saffron, salt, bay leaf and knob of ginger. Pour in enough cold water to leave just the top of the breast sticking out. Cover with a lid and bring to a simmer, then turn down the heat so that only the odd bubble can be seen. Cook gently for about 1½ hours, or until the meat juices run clear. Take the chicken out of the pan (keep the stock for a soup or sauce for another dish) and set aside until cool enough to handle. While still lukewarm, remove the meat from the carcass in bite-sized pieces.

To make the sauce, put the mango chutney and apricots into a large bowl. Toast the curry powder in a dry frying pan until aromatic, a few seconds only, then add the chopped ginger. Stir briefly, then add both to the bowl, followed by the Worcestershire sauce, mayonnaise and yoghurt. Season to taste.

Fold the cooled chicken through the sauce and chill for 2 hours. Bring back to room temperature for serving. At that point, fold through most of the coriander and serve topped with the almonds and the coriander sprigs. Serve in a border of rice with a crisp green salad.

Chicken with fried rice

The chicken in this recipe is cooked in almost exactly the same way as in Coronation Chicken (see page 97), but with different flavourings in the poaching water. Here I use the hugely flavourful stock as the sauce, just as it is after straining. I quite often serve the chicken simply with boiled rice and a vast green salad. Sometimes, though, it is more exciting to fry the rice, especially for adults (and it's apparently more digestible). Here my favourite flavouring ingredients – garlic, ginger and chilli – add a punch, but you could also stir in beaten egg, sliced mushrooms, cubes of green and red pepper for colour, peas, water chestnuts … the possibilities are endless.

Serves 6

1 chicken, about 1.5kg
1 lemon or lime, halved
2 onions, peeled and halved
1 chicken stock cube
75ml dry white
2 tbsp soy sauce
4 garlic cloves, unpeeled
40g fresh root ginger, peeled and
    roughly chopped
1 fresh red chilli, halved lengthways
    if you like a kick of heat
1 tsp black peppercorns
salt

FOR THE FRIED RICE
350g basmati rice
1 tsp coconut oil
1 bay leaf (optional)
6 cardamom pods (optional)
1 tbsp sesame oil or coconut oil
2 garlic cloves, peeled and sliced
1 x 40g piece of fresh root ginger,
    peeled and cut into matchsticks
1 fresh red chilli, finely chopped
small bunch of fresh coriander

Put the chicken, breast-side down, in a large pan or ovenproof casserole dish that is quite a tight fit. Put the halved lemon in the cavity. Tuck all the remaining ingredients in and around the chicken, then pour in enough cold water to leave only the tip of the chicken showing. Cover with the lid and place in the roasting oven of the Aga for about 45 minutes, then remove from the heat, turn the chicken over, and leave it to rest in the liquid for at least an hour. Without an Aga, cover with a lid and bring to the boil on the hob. Turn the heat down low and simmer, still covered, for about 1 hour, turning over halfway through.

Start cooking your rice an hour or so before the chicken will be ready. Rinse it briefly first in a sieve to get rid of excess starch. I then put it in my rice cooker with coconut oil, salt and pepper and the recommended amount of water (usually double the measure of rice). I sometimes add a bay leaf and cardamom pods for extra flavour. I switch the machine on and it then does everything.

If you don't have a rice cooker, start cooking the rice about 15 minutes before you're going to eat. Put the rice into a pan with double its volume of water. Add the flavourings, cover with a lid and bring to the boil. Once boiling, turn the heat down low and simmer for 10–12 minutes. Drain well and fluff up with a fork.

When the chicken is ready, remove it from the liquid, drain well and place on a board. When cool enough to handle, take the meat off the bones as neatly as possible and arrange on a serving platter. Pour a ladleful or two of the stock over the top, cover and keep warm. You'll have lots of stock left over, but see tip below.

To finish the rice, heat the oil in a large frying pan and fry the garlic, ginger and chilli for about 1 minute – no longer or the garlic will burn and taste bitter. Add the boiled rice to the pan and stir-fry until it is hot and the flavourings are well combined. Roughly chop the coriander leaves and finely chop the stalks. Add the stalks and most of the leaves to the pan. Stir well again, then serve straight away with the remaining coriander leaves sprinkled on top and the poached chicken.

⧽ TIP ⧼

There'll be lots of rich stock left over from this recipe, so cool it in a sealable container and chill overnight. The next day, skim off the fat. Use the stock as the base of a soup, or reduce it for future use: pour it into a pan, bring to the boil and simmer until reduced to your liking. Once cool, freeze in well-labelled containers.

Chapter 4

Children & Fussy Eaters

Six months after I met Ben, I met his sons Orion and Hal, who were aged five and two. They ate chicken goujons, cucumber sticks, hummus, sausages and, on a good day, an omelette, but that was about it. They were difficult to feed for many years, which I quite understand now, but then I was just too emotional. They were shell-shocked because of the breakdown of their parents' marriage, I was a new person in their lives – the wicked stepmother – and I would be (nervously) cooking things that looked different and tasted different from what they were used to. I should have been less anxious, but I wasn't and that is when the rot set in.

If I had my time over again, I would never cook anything different for the children. They are just the same as adults in having distinct likes and dislikes, but making 'kids' food' is often a mistake. I did, though, and created a rod for my back. I recently found myself pondering this when I had lunch with my best friend Claire and her small son Luis, who ate exactly what we did. I wondered if this was down to nature or nurture. Did she just get a good eater?

A classic case of children exerting power through refusing food happened not long after I had met Hal and Orion. My friend Katie was staying with us in Devon and she kindly made her delicious bolognese sauce for the crowd we had to lunch that day. There were ten children sitting around the kitchen table wolfing down the pasta, all except Orion and Hal, who flatly refused to touch it. I bellowed at them, then left the room and burst into tears. Nearly a year into being a step-parent, I was at my wits' end when it came to mealtimes, and my kitchen could not have been less happy. But when I returned to the kitchen, Katie had persuaded the boys to eat. That was an object lesson – children can play up when mother (or stepmother) is around, but allow themselves to be persuaded by another. It is still happening. On a recent holiday in Morocco, the food was delicious, but I got sulky looks when I put a little morsel of each wonderful dish on their plates. When I was absent one lunchtime, my friend reported that the kids had eaten up without a quibble: 'Of course they ate ... you weren't there.'

Of the four boys that I feed regularly, one likes red meat and anything sweet, the second likes anything white – cheese, egg, bread, pasta, potatoes – but has come round to red meat, though is not a big fan of anything exotic. Bay, my eldest, loves fish and anything spicy, but won't touch fruit. Oscar's food tastes are unclear because he enjoys making a fuss more than he enjoys eating, but I suspect, given a choice, he would live off mango smoothies, bagels and raspberry jam.

Aged two, Oscar developed eczema, and when my doctor told me that childhood eczema was sometimes helped by adopting a wheat-free, dairy-free diet, my heart sank. Coping with that, and catering for the various tastes of the older three, was my culinary low point. Even now, I don't feel I have cracked the fussy-eater dilemma. Fortunately, there are a few recipes that they will all eat, which I have included in this chapter.

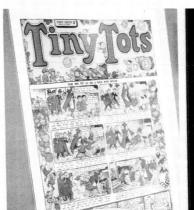

Heather's bang-bang chicken

During the school term, when I'm often away filming and Ben is working late, my kids don't just fend for themselves. We have an amazing nanny called Heather, who came to us when Bay, now ten, was a baby. Heather didn't cook much when she first arrived, but over the years she has grown keener and keener on cooking, and is one of the inspirations for this book. I know through Heather's experience, and my own, that cooks aren't all born; many people develop an interest in food much later in life.

This is a recipe that Heather found in the charity cookbook published by the boys' school, and it was a massive hit with everyone from the first.

Serves 2–3

2 skinless, boneless chicken breasts
2 slices of white bread
2 handfuls of grated Cheddar or any
   hard cheese

1 tbsp roughly chopped parsley
1 large egg
olive oil
salt and freshly ground black pepper

Cut the chicken breasts into strips about 1cm wide.

Put the bread, cheese and parsley into a food processor and blend until the bread is crumbly and everything is combined. Put the mixture in a bowl.

Break the egg into another bowl and beat with a fork until well mixed, seasoning with salt and pepper.

Dip the chicken first into the egg, and then into the breadcrumbs until well coated.

Heat a generous amount of oil in a frying pan and fry the coated chicken for about 2–3 minutes on each side, depending on how thick the pieces are. Serve straight away.

Fish goujons

Basically these are fish fingers, very easy to make and much nicer than bought or frozen fish fingers. My younger boys like eating these goujons, and are very keen on helping me to make them, measuring out the ingredients and so on, which I think is good for their maths. I often have a big session with the boys, then freeze the prepared goujons for another time.

They are good made with cod, although I used to make them with monkfish, which was meatier. This was the only way I could get fish into my fish-hating stepsons, making it look as if it were something else. Another trick I employed to get them used to fishy flavours was chucking anchovies into a number of other dishes: a tomato sauce with some anchovies in it doesn't taste at all fishy, just more intense in flavour.

Serves 6

6 tbsp jumbo oats
6 tbsp ground almonds
50g Parmesan cheese, freshly grated
1–2 tbsp finely chopped chives
700g fillet of cod or haddock

plain flour
1 large egg
olive oil or sunflower oil, for frying
salt and freshly ground black pepper

Put the oats, almonds and Parmesan into a food processor and whizz until the mixture is chopped but still with a little texture in it. Tip into a shallow bowl and stir in the chives.

Cut the fish into finger-sized pieces – they should be about 2 fingers wide and about the length of your middle finger.

Put a couple of tablespoons of flour into a clean bowl and season well. Crack the egg into another, similar-sized bowl, add seasoning and beat together.

Preheat the oven to 100°C/Fan 80°C/Gas ½.

Meanwhile, take each piece of fish and dip first into the flour, then into the egg, then into the oat mixture. Set aside on a plate. Once all the pieces are coated, heat a little oil in a large frying pan. When hot, fry the goujons 3 or 4 at a time until crisp and golden all over. Transfer to a baking sheet and keep warm in the oven.

Cook the other goujons in the same way. Serve with salad and new potatoes tossed in butter.

Mac 'n' cheese

Last summer, for a big event at my sons' school, there were festival-style food vans, which is how I came across Anna Mae's extraordinary mac 'n' cheese van. Notting Hill mums, who to my certain knowledge have not eaten a carbohydrate for over a decade, were going back for seconds! This is magic food that can cheer up the most heartbroken teen, and it travels well, so can be taken to anyone in need of solace.

Serves 4–6

300g macaroni
5g butter
1 slice of white bread, made into crumbs
3–4 tbsp freshly grated Parmesan cheese
3–4 medium tomatoes, sliced
salt and freshly ground black pepper

FOR THE CHEESE SAUCE
40g butter
40g plain flour
600ml milk
freshly grated nutmeg
1 tsp English mustard powder
100g mature Cheddar cheese, grated

Cook the macaroni in a pan of boiling salted water until al dente. That should take about 8–10 minutes, or follow the timings on the packet.

Meanwhile, make the cheese sauce. In a medium pan, melt the butter over a low heat. Gradually sprinkle in the flour, stirring until it is a smooth paste and beginning to bubble. Slowly add the milk, stirring continuously until the sauce is smooth and has thickened slightly. Add a grating of nutmeg, the mustard and most of the Cheddar and stir until the sauce is creamy. Season with salt and pepper.

Preheat the grill and grease a large baking dish with the butter. Drain the macaroni, then mix it into the cheese sauce. Pour into the prepared baking dish.

Put the breadcrumbs into a bowl with the Parmesan and remaining Cheddar, toss together and season. Arrange the tomato slices on top of the pasta, then sprinkle over the breadcrumb mixture. Grill until golden and bubbling, turning it to brown the top evenly. Allow to stand for 5 minutes before serving.

⤜ VARIATION ⤛

For an even faster option, drain the pasta, leaving a little of the water in the pan. Spoon in a tablespoon of ricotta followed by a lot of very finely grated Cheddar (I use a fine Microplane so that it is even finer than Parmesan). This melts immediately into the hot pasta, and is the quickest ever macaroni cheese, complete in just 10 minutes. (Don't do this with gnocchi, though, it doesn't work.)

Oscar's pesto sauce

I have already acknowledged making a rod for my back by cooking different things for all four boys, so it won't surprise you to hear that one of my stock dishes is called 'pasta with three sauces'. I offer this one, plus the tomato sauce and carbonara sauce that appear after this recipe, or sometimes the very cheesy sauce from the macaroni recipe on page 109, or the bolognese sauce from page 115.

My children love pesto, and Oscar's version is particularly cheesy, as that is how he likes it. You can use leaves other than basil, such as parsley, rocket or spinach, and other nuts – maybe walnuts – instead of the pine nuts. I have a friend who, desperate to get green veg into her children, cooks broccoli until soft, then crushes it with a tablespoon of jarred pesto and garlic. It looks just like pesto, even if the taste is not entirely authentic, but it works with some kids if you go gently at first.

Serves 4–6
3 handfuls fresh basil leaves (I tend to use the smaller-leaved Greek basil)
50g pine nuts, lightly toasted
1 garlic clove, peeled
75g Parmesan or pecorino cheese, freshly grated
100–125ml olive oil
salt and freshly ground black pepper

Put the basil leaves into your food processor or blender, then add the pine kernels, garlic and cheese. Blend until the leaves are finely chopped.

Pour in the oil and blend until it becomes thick. Season to taste and it's ready.

Quick tomato sauce

The fresh tomatoes used in this recipe are barely cooked, thus retaining more of their goodness, and the basic sauce can be varied in quite a few ways. I don't add onion, but you can if you like – perhaps a large white one chopped very, very finely and cooked at the same time as the garlic. You could also add some chopped fresh chilli or dried chilli flakes to give the sauce a kick. Serve it over pasta with a sprinkling of torn basil leaves.

Serves 4–6

750g fresh plum tomatoes, small or large
2 tbsp olive oil
4 garlic cloves, peeled and finely sliced
salt and freshly ground black pepper

Use a sharp knife to remove the calyx and hard core from the tomatoes, then chop coarsely. (I don't bother skinning them, but if you want to, put them in a bowl of boiling water for about 30 seconds, then into cold water. Drain and slip the skins off before chopping.)

Heat the olive oil in a large, heavy-based pan and fry the garlic very gently for about 1–2 minutes, just until you can start to smell its aroma. Add the tomatoes and fry gently for another 5 minutes. Season to taste with salt and pepper.

Bolognese sauce

I once cooked a truly authentic bolognese ragù – I think the recipe came from the *Guardian* – but the children wouldn't touch it. It was very rich and dense, made with beef and chicken livers. It came in handy for dinner that night, though. As a change from pasta, I par-cooked some potatoes, put them in with the meat and baked them together in the Aga. Delicious!

The beef sauce in the Lasagne on page 88 can be used as a bolognese sauce, but this one here is specifically for children, using the briefly cooked tomatoes of the sauce on page 112. The flavours are simple and much more to children's taste.

You can add fried bacon bits to the basic sauce if you like, and if your children don't like identifiable onion, chop it very, very finely in a food processor. While this sauce is obviously good with pasta, I also serve it with rice and on top of baked potatoes. Sprinkle with some grated cheese for extra flavour.

Serves 4–6

2 tbsp olive oil
1 onion, peeled and very finely diced
1 carrot, very finely diced
1 celery stick, very finely diced
400g minced beef
about 300ml water

1 tbsp tomato purée
a few dried chilli flakes (optional)
about ½ quantity of my Quick Tomato
    Sauce (see page 112)
salt and freshly ground black pepper

Heat the olive oil in a large pan and add the onion, carrot and celery. Fry gently for about 10 minutes, until they have softened.

Add the mince and fry, turning often, until it has browned. Add the water, tomato purée and chilli flakes (if using). Season well, stir together and bubble, uncovered, for 20 minutes. The liquid should virtually disappear.

Now all you have to do is add the tomato sauce to the pan and mix well over a medium heat until hot. Serve with your pasta.

My quick carbonara

There are days when I don't want to cook, or I haven't planned a meal ahead, or I have unexpected guests, and on these days this recipe saves me because it doesn't look lazy and is amazing comfort food. I usually make a quick tomato salad while the pasta is boiling, or have some spinach on the side, but, to be honest, I have yet to sell the boys on the joys of spinach.

I learnt how to make this dish from Ben's aunt, who lives on a hill in Tuscany with twelve show dachshunds. When her nephew, four hungry boys and I squeezed out of a Fiat 500 one day (it was the only rental car left at Florence airport), she rustled up spaghetti carbonara in minutes, while handing out large drinks at the same time.

Using a large bowl and doing things in the following order are part of how the recipe works so well and can be done so quickly.

Serves 4–6

250g bacon or pancetta, chopped
  or cubed
500g spaghetti
3 large egg yolks
80ml double cream

1 large garlic clove, peeled
at least 50g Parmesan or pecorino cheese,
  finely grated
salt and freshly ground black pepper

Put the frying pan over a medium heat. When hot, fry the bacon until brown and crisp.

Fill a large saucepan with boiling salted water and cook the pasta until al dente, about 10–12 minutes, or according to the timing on the packet.

Put the egg yolks in a bowl with the cream, salt and pepper. Stick the garlic clove on the end of a fork and use to gently mix the contents of the bowl.

Grate the cheese into a large bowl. Drain the cooked bacon on some kitchen paper, then add it to the cheese.

When the pasta is cooked, drain well and place on top of the cheese and bacon. Leave for a minute, then pour the egg and cream mixture over the pasta and mix really well. Serve straight away.

(*Rupert and the*) stuffed baked potatoes

From a book called *Lots of Fun to Cook with Rupert* (recipes by Sonia Allison), these potatoes were one of the first things I ever learnt to make when I was a child. I tried all twelve recipes in the book, but the potato one I still do, although I've made many changes to it over the intervening years.

You too can make changes: perhaps include cheese in the potato mixture instead of sprinkling it on top, or leave out the eggs, although I do like the children to have eggs as often as possible. You could also serve a variation on these skins for breakfast. Scoop out the middle of the potatoes, leaving a wall of flesh about 1cm thick. Crack an egg into the hole, scatter the top with cooked crumbled bacon, then pop back into the oven until the egg has set. In our house a 'full English' is one potato skin served with some home-baked beans (see page 124).

A great thing about stuffed baked potatoes is that, provided you don't add the egg white, they can be frozen, which is very handy when cooking for a lot of people.

Serves 6

8 large baking potatoes, washed and dried
50g butter, plus a little extra for greasing
2 tbsp milk
4 eggs, separated

3 tbsp chopped chives
freshly grated nutmeg
100g Cheddar or other hard cheese, grated
salt and freshly ground black pepper

Preheat the oven to 200°C/Fan 180°C/Gas 6. Butter a baking sheet and put the potatoes on it. Season with a little salt. Prick the skins with a fork in a couple of places. Bake for 1–1½ hours, until the skin is crisp and the inside soft.

Set the potatoes aside until cool enough to handle, then cut in half lengthways and scoop the flesh into a bowl. Put the skins back on the baking sheet and keep warm.

Add the butter and milk to the bowl of potato and mash quite roughly. Stir in the egg yolks and chives, and season to taste with salt, pepper and nutmeg.

Whip up the egg whites until firm. Using a metal tablespoon, fold them into the potato mixture. Pile this into the potato skins: I use only six (one per person), as I like the potato to be really piled up. Las Vegas skins!

Sprinkle the cheese over the top of your little potato soufflés and put back into the oven at 200°C/Fan 180°C/Gas 6 for 15–20 minutes. Serve hot, perhaps with a slice of ham, some salad and chutney (always chutney); ideal at Christmas, for instance.

Gyozas (Japanese dumplings)

These dumplings are fried, then steamed, and taste wonderful. My children love them. The filling below uses prawns, but you can make a filling from whatever you like; cabbage and spiced pork are traditional. All the chopping and cutting of the ingredients can be done in a blender or processor.

Makes about 50

1 bunch of fresh coriander, very finely chopped
500g cooked peeled prawns
1 x 3cm piece of fresh root ginger, peeled and grated
3 garlic cloves, peeled and grated
8 spring onions, very finely chopped
1 x 284g packet gyoza wrappers

sunflower oil, for frying
3 tbsp water

FOR THE DIPPING SAUCE
60ml soy sauce
½ tsp sesame oil
40ml rice vinegar

Put the coriander, prawns, ginger, garlic and spring onions into the bowl of a food processor. Blend until the mixture is finely chopped. Take care not to overdo it – you don't want it to turn to mush.

Fill a small glass with water. Lay a few wrappers out on a board and put a teaspoonful of the prawn mixture in the centre of each one. Dip your finger into the water, then run it around the edge of a wrapper, dipping it in the water again if necessary to complete the circle. Pick up two sides of the wrapper at the middle and loosely hold them together without securing. Make 3 small pleats in the curved side nearest you, working from the middle out to the right edge and pressing them as you go. Now make another 3 pleats from the middle to the left edge. Press the pleated side against the unpleated side to secure in a classic half-moon shape. Do the same with the other wrappers and set aside. Continue this process in small batches until you've shaped all the dumplings. (If you need more help, YouTube has lots of videos showing how to do this whole step.)

You will need to cook the dumplings in batches, so heat 1 teaspoon sunflower oil in a large non-stick frying pan over a medium heat. Fry 10–12 until golden and crisp on the flat side. Add the water – stand back as it may spit – then put a lid on the pan. Steam-cook the dumplings for a further 3–4 minutes, by which time the water should have evaporated, and the dumplings completely cooked. Keep warm while you cook the remaining gyozas in the same way. To make the sauce, simply mix the ingredients together in a bowl. Offer with the dumplings. Some Asian Tomato & Chilli Chutney (see page 204) also goes well with them.

Pizza

In some form or another, pizza features large in our family life. We often have what we call 'pizza toast' – a slice of toast spread with tomato purée and topped with grated Cheddar or mozzarella, which then goes briefly into the roasting oven of the Aga. It's perfect for a snack after a long day, or when we arrive in Devon after the trip from London.

We also do proper pizzas on the pizza stone in our Big Green Egg, a ceramic outdoor oven. That's Ben's province. I make the pizza dough (my own version of a Jamie Oliver recipe) and then everyone can choose what they want to put on top. The first time I did it I bought olives, anchovies, salami, the lot, but the boys went for cheese in the main, preferring pre-grated mozzarella for some reason. Oscar actually piled his pizza high with canned sweetcorn.

Makes 6

1kg strong white bread flour, or 800g flour
    plus 200g fine semolina flour, plus extra
    for dusting
1 tsp fine salt
2 x 7g sachets of dried yeast
1 tbsp caster sugar
4 tbsp extra virgin olive oil
650ml lukewarm water

FOR THE TOPPINGS
Quick Tomato Sauce (see page 112),
    or some passata
anything else you like, e.g. mozzarella
    cheese, olives, basil, salami, green or red
    pepper strips, artichoke hearts, olives,
    anchovies, eggs
olive oil, for drizzling

Sift the flour and salt into a large bowl and make a well in the centre.

Put the yeast, sugar and olive oil into a jug, add the water and set aside for a few minutes. Pour the mixture into the well in the flour.

Using a fork in a circular motion, slowly bring the flour from the sides into the water. Continue mixing until a sticky dough forms. When you can't use your fork any more, flour your hands and pat the dough into a ball.

Lightly flour a work surface and knead the dough for 6–10 minutes, until it is smooth. Roll into a ball.

Clean and flour the large bowl, then put the dough in it. Cover with a tea towel and leave in a warm place for about 1 hour. It should at least double in size.

CONTINUED OVERLEAF ❯

Take the risen dough out of the bowl, place it on a lightly floured work surface and punch the air out (what they call 'knocking back'). Knead it lightly, then use it straight away, or wrap in clingfilm and keep in the fridge (or freezer) until needed.

When ready to cook, heat the oven to 230°C/Fan 210°C/Gas 8 and put a baking sheet or two inside to heat up. Alternatively, heat your lidded barbecue and/or pizza stone.

Divide the dough into 6 equal pieces and roll each one into a ball. Using your hands (as Italians do) or a rolling pin (as I do), stretch or roll out each ball into a circle about 5mm thick. It's a good idea to keep the perimeter a bit thicker than the middle so that your toppings won't slide off.

Top first with some tomato sauce, then add anything else you want, preferably including cheese, which melts so deliciously over everything. I think this is why the boys like making pizzas so much: they are choosing what to cook for themselves, and the oven transforms it into something very different.

Drizzle each pizza with olive oil and, using a couple of fish slices – or a pizza paddle if you have one – transfer them to the hot baking sheet or pizza stone. Bake for 10–15 minutes. Enjoy!

'Baked' beans in tomato sauce

I love Heinz baked beans, but my children don't, which I think is very strange. Luckily, they do like my homemade version, which contains less salt and sugar, but still tastes good.

Authentic American baked beans would include salted bacon or pork belly, as well as treacle or molasses. I think this plainer version is better.

Serves 4–6

250-275g dried haricot beans, or 2 x 400g tins haricot beans, drained and rinsed (other beans can be used if you like, but avoid black or red ones)
2 tbsp olive oil
3 garlic cloves, peeled and crushed
1 carrot, peeled and very finely chopped

1 celery stick, very finely chopped
400g fresh plum tomatoes, roughly chopped
2 tbsp tomato purée
150–200ml vegetable stock
salt and freshly ground black pepper

If using dried beans, you'll need to soak them overnight. Put them into a large bowl and pour in enough cold water to cover them very generously. There needs to be a couple of centimetres of water above them as they will swell. The next day, drain the beans well. Transfer to a large saucepan, then cover the beans again with fresh water. Put a lid on the pan and bring to the boil. Skim off any scum and turn the heat down to a simmer. Partially cover and leave to simmer for about 1½ hours (depending how old the beans are). They should be just tender, not breaking up.

Meanwhile, make the tomato sauce. Heat the oil in a medium pan and fry the garlic for a few minutes. Add the carrot and celery, turn the heat down and cook gently until softened, about 15–20 minutes.

Add the tomatoes, tomato purée and stock, and stir everything together. Bring to the boil, then simmer for about 10 minutes. Purée with a stick blender, or cool a little before blitzing in a blender or food processor.

Drain the cooked beans well, then pour into the pan of tomato sauce. Season to taste with salt and pepper, and simmer for another 10–15 minutes.

Rösti potatoes

These delicious potato cakes hail from Switzerland, and they have conquered the world – and my children. They can be made with floury or waxy potatoes, such as Maris Piper or Charlotte, which can be used raw or parboiled. (If parboiling, peel the potatoes and boil them whole until just tender, not soft, then drain and chill for a couple of hours before grating.) You could add shards of cooked bacon and onion to the potato mix, and fry the potato cakes in butter or goose or duck fat if you want a richer flavour.

Serve the röstis with smoked ham, Swiss cheese, or a poached or fried egg on top. Alternatively, serve like blinis, with smoked salmon or salmon roe topped with soured cream, chopped spring onion and dill. The cakes have a lovely texture, and I think they are great for breakfast or a satisfying supper.

Serves 4–6

450g Maris Piper potatoes
olive oil, for frying
salt and freshly ground black pepper

Peel the potatoes and grate them coarsely. Lay them out on a clean tea towel, then gather up the edges of the cloth and squeeze out all the starch and moisture. When as dry as possible, season the potato with salt and pepper and mix well.

Press a handful of potato inside a 6–7cm pastry cutter. Carefully remove the cutter and the potato should hold its form nicely.

Heat a generous amount of olive oil in a frying pan. Using a spatula, carefully lift each potato cake into the pan. Fry for 3–4 minutes on each side, slipping them over once or twice, until golden brown.

Drain on kitchen paper and serve.

Homemade oven chips

Chips cooked in the oven need very little oil, so are much healthier than those deep-fried. And the bigger your chips are cut, the healthier they will be too, as they absorb less oil than the small surface area of thin French fries. Also, there's no need to peel the potatoes – many of the nutrients, including fibre and potassium, are in or near the skin, so cooking them unpeeled is a healthier option.

Different flavourings can be added to your basic potatoes before baking them. Try celery salt, or a mixture of ground cumin and coriander, or some chopped thyme leaves, or even some crushed garlic.

Serves 4

1kg good chip potatoes, such as Maris Piper, King Edward or Desirée
2 tbsp olive oil
salt and freshly ground black pepper

Preheat the oven to 220°C/Fan 200°C/Gas 7, and place a non-stick baking sheet inside to warm up.

Scrub or peel the potatoes. Cut them into chips 1–2cm thick. Put them in a pan of cold water, cover with a lid and bring to the boil. Simmer for 3 minutes, then drain well. Return to the pan, add the oil and season well.

Tip the chips onto the hot baking sheet, shaking lightly to get them into a single layer with no overlapping. Bake for about 20–30 minutes, turning them over occasionally, until golden brown and crisp.

Serve hot, perhaps with an extra sprinkling of salt.

Chapter 5

Baking

Baking is great fun, and I have tried my hand at making many things over the years. I love the combining of ingredients, watching things blossom in the oven, and seeing the pleasure with which people eat the end results. Baking is quite a precise art, which took me time to learn, but gives great satisfaction.

To be honest, I seldom eat what I bake, as I am so often being careful about my weight. Most of the stuff I bake is for school events, such as Christmas fairs, summer fêtes, Red Nose days, charity coffee mornings, jumble sales and cake competitions. Every school does similar things, and it is very satisfying and enjoyable to make stuff that people can appreciate and that will make money for a good cause at the same time.

One such school occasion was when we were clearing a scrubby piece of land at the back of the boys' school, which was going to be made into a woodland play area. They had called for volunteers, and as I live quite near, I thought I could provide a few Thermoses of coffee and perhaps some cake. I put out a plea on Twitter for a good recipe, and – as I say on page 144 – Jack Monroe answered, giving me permission to use her Guinness and Chocolate Brownies. I didn't taste a single one because they disappeared as soon as they were produced. I heard, though, that they were delicious!

I also like the idea of getting the children to help me bake something, which, prettily wrapped and tied with ribbon, they can then present to their teacher. And why not do the same thing for grandmothers', aunts' or friends' birthdays? My boys love to bake, and, as I have said elsewhere, learning to use recipes is fantastically educational. It involves maths and science, but is a family activity, so much better than homework. They particularly like 'helping' with Rocky Road (page 134), but I fear more of the ingredients disappear into their eager mouths than go into the mixing bowl.

We made a whole TV programme about the popularity of baking competitions at agricultural and county shows; they attract many entrants of all ages. When we did *Handmade Britain*, the idea was that I would learn how to do something I hadn't done before, and then enter a competition, in one case for afternoon tea. For this event, I learnt to make scones, jam and chocolate éclairs. Richard Hunt, a professional chef who has since become a friend for life, taught me how to make scones, while Victoria Cranfield showed me the secret of damson jam. I actually came second, and both recipes appear in this book (see pages 143 and 29).

My sister Sofie bakes a lot – brownies, cookies, big beautiful cakes for family and other celebrations – and one of her recipes features in this chapter (see page 148). In fact, she is the true baker in the family.

Rocky road

Everyone loves Rocky Road, a delightfully knobbly mixture of biscuit, marshmallow, honeycomb and chocolate that is so much fun to make at home, especially for children. They like measuring everything, melting the chocolate, and eating most of the ingredients before they ever get to the mixing bowl!

You can use just dark chocolate, or a mixture of dark and milk chocolate (as below), which creates something that is still toothsome but not too sweet. Kids often prefer the texture and taste of it.

Makes 24 squares

175g unsalted butter
4 tbsp golden syrup
175g dark chocolate
100g milk chocolate
150g digestive biscuits, broken into small pieces but not crumbs

150g rich tea biscuits, broken into small pieces but not crumbs
100g mini marshmallows
50g Maltesers

Line a 20–21cm square cake tin with baking parchment.

Put the butter, syrup and both types of chocolate in a large pan over a low heat and melt together, stirring every now and then to mix well. You should end up with a really smooth and silky mixture.

Add the biscuits and half the marshmallows to the pan and mix thoroughly.

Spoon into the lined tin and press down using the back of a wooden spoon. Scatter over the remaining marshmallows and the Maltesers and press down to make sure they stick to the warm chocolate mixture.

Refrigerate for at least 5 or 6 hours, preferably overnight, until hard. Cut into squares and enjoy!

Ginger biscuits

I love the flavour of ginger, using it in savoury dishes almost as much as I do chillies. But I do like a good ginger biscuit, my affection stemming from the time I used to make gingerbread men from my favourite Rupert Bear cookbook. You could do that with this recipe too, adding raisins or chocolate chips to make the faces. These biscuits are very handy to keep in an airtight box, ready for when people pop in for morning coffee or tea.

While the soothing medicinal properties of ginger are well known, please don't tell anyone with morning sickness, which I had, that a ginger biscuit will sort them out. That's just wishful thinking.

Makes
about 27

125g unsalted butter
175g caster sugar
1 large egg
3 balls of stem ginger (about 65g in total), chopped

1 tbsp stem ginger syrup, from the jar
250g plain flour
1 tsp baking powder
1 tsp bicarbonate of soda
1 tbsp ground ginger

Preheat the oven to 170°C/Fan 150°C/Gas 3. Line 3 baking sheets with baking parchment.

In a large bowl, cream the butter and sugar together until smooth, then gradually beat in the egg. Chop the stem ginger and add to the bowl along with the ginger syrup, flour, baking powder, bicarbonate of soda and ground ginger. Stir well with a wooden spoon until the mixture forms a dough. Scoop up a teaspoonful of dough, roll into a ball between your hands, then place on a prepared baking sheet. Continue doing this until the dough has been used up; you should have about 27 balls. Remember, they will spread during baking, so keep them well spaced.

Bake for 12–15 minutes, until golden around the edges, rotating the trays halfway through so that they brown evenly.

Let the biscuits cool and firm up a little on the tray, then place on a wire rack to become cold. Store in an airtight container for up to 5 days.

Chocolate & beetroot cake

We were in Ireland for *Location, Location, Location*, and went to a lovely house that was for sale. The lady had a small at-home shop, and she left us some beetroot chocolate brownies, which were unbelievably good. As the couple didn't buy the house, I felt too embarrasssed to ask the owner for the recipe, so when I came home I went online and found this. It is a Nigel Slater recipe, and is absolutely delicious. I have made it ever since.

Don't let any child who doesn't like beetroot see you using it as they won't eat the cake, swearing they can taste it. I swear 100 per cent that you can't. What the beetroot does is give an amazing moistness and richness. Clever, lovely Nigel.

Serves 8

250g beetroot

200g butter, plus a little extra for greasing

200g dark chocolate (70% cocoa solids), broken into pieces

4 tbsp hot espresso coffee

135g plain flour

1 heaped tsp baking powder

3 tbsp good-quality cocoa powder

5 eggs

190g golden caster sugar

TO SERVE

crème fraîche

poppy seeds

First cook the beetroot, whole and unpeeled, in boiling unsalted water for about 30–40 minutes, depending on size. Test for readiness by inserting a sharp knife point: the beetroot should feel soft. Drain and cool under running cold water. Peel, slice out the stem and root, then blitz the flesh to a purée in a food processor or blender.

Preheat the oven to 180°C/Fan 160°C/Gas 4. Lightly butter a 20cm loose-bottomed cake tin and line the base with a circle of baking parchment.

Put the chocolate in a small bowl set over a pan of simmering water. Leave to melt without stirring. When melted, pour the hot coffee over it and stir once. Add the butter and push the pieces gently under the surface and leave to soften.

Sift the flour, baking powder and cocoa into a large bowl. Put the egg whites and yolks in separate bowls. Stir the yolks together.

Working quickly but gently, remove the bowl of chocolate from the heat and stir until the butter has combined with the chocolate. Leave for a few moments, then stir in the egg yolks. Do this quickly, mixing firmly. Fold in the beetroot purée.

Whisk the egg whites until stiff, then fold in the sugar using a metal spoon. Using the same spoon, fold this mixture into the beetroot bowl. Do not overmix. Fold in the flour mixture.

Quickly pour the batter into the prepared tin and put in the oven, immediately lowering the temperature to 170°C/Fan 150°C/Gas 3. Bake for 40 minutes. The rim of the cake should feel spongy, while the inner part should still wobble a little when gently shaken.

Leave it to cool (it will sink a tad in the centre), loosening it around the edges with a palette knife after half an hour or so. Don't remove from the tin until it is completely cold.

Nigel serves his cake in thick slices, with crème fraîche and poppy seeds.

Scones

Richard Hunt, consultant chef and a partner in The Devon Scone Company, is (obviously) an expert scone-maker – apparently, he started baking them when he was only six years old. I met him through a show we made called *Handmade Britain*. This is his recipe, which has become mine.

When I don't have buttermilk – it's occasionally difficult to find – I add half a tablespoon of lemon juice or white wine vinegar to 125ml milk. This sours the milk a little, coming near to the delicious flavour of buttermilk. According to Richard, the buttermilk adds flavour, but the acid also helps the dough to rise.

Makes 8–9

250g plain flour
35g caster sugar
1 tsp baking powder
35g milk powder

30g butter
125ml buttermilk
¼ tsp salt
1 medium egg, beaten, to glaze

Preheat the oven to 220°C/Fan 200°C/Gas 7 and line a baking sheet with baking parchment.

Put the flour, sugar, baking powder, milk powder and butter in a large bowl. Rub together with your fingertips so that the mixture turns cream-coloured and slightly crumbly. The odd fleck of butter is not a bad thing.

Add the buttermilk and salt, stir well, then bring together with your hands to form a firm ball of dough.

Knead the dough very lightly for 10–15 seconds, no more, otherwise it will be tough, then press it out with your hands to a thickness of 4cm. Don't flour your hands or the work surface while doing this; you don't want any more flour.

Using a 6cm cutter, stamp out 8–9 circles – a quick downward cut without twisting will give you the best rise in the oven. By the ninth one, you might have to reshape the dough trimmings by hand to make a final circle.

Place the scones on the prepared baking sheet, a few centimetres apart. Brush the tops with the beaten egg, then bake for 15–20 minutes, until risen and lightly coloured. Serve warm with jam and lashings of clotted cream on top for a wonderful Devon cream tea.

Guinness & chocolate brownies

I have done *Question Time* on BBC television four times because I have this weird belief that it's good to do things that frighten us. The last time I popped up on the panel I was alongside Jack Monroe. We'd never met before, but I already knew her food writing and was thrilled to meet her. A few months later I signed up to spend a Saturday morning clearing out a new woodland play area at the back of the boys' school. I thought coffee and cake might be in order, and Jack sent me this recipe, which I made in batches. I never tasted them, however, as every brownie I produced was consumed with an enthusiasm for sweet treats you don't usually see amongst Notting Hill mums.

Makes 24

oil, for greasing (optional)
250ml Guinness
200g dark chocolate, broken into
    small pieces
200g butter, cubed
3 eggs

300g caster sugar
pinch of salt
150g plain flour
100g milk chocolate, broken
    into small pieces

Preheat the oven to 180°C/Fan 160°C/Gas 4. Use a little oil to grease a shallow 30 x 20cm baking tin, or line it with baking parchment. Pour the Guinness into a small pan and place over a low to medium heat. Perch a mixing bowl on top, add the dark chocolate and butter, and allow to melt together, stirring occasionally.

Meanwhile, break your eggs into a bowl, add the sugar and salt, and whisk together until well combined. Gradually add the flour, a quarter at a time, and beat it all in before adding the next batch.

When the melted chocolate and butter have combined, very gradually beat them into the flour and egg mixture. Now it is time to add the hot Guinness, which should have reduced by half (125ml instead of 250ml). Gradually pour it into the chocolate mixture, mixing well all the time. It will be very runny – Jack says it looks like 'brownie soup'.

Pour the batter into the prepared tin, then poke the little milk chocolate pieces into it at random intervals. Bake on the middle shelf of the oven for 40 minutes, and don't be tempted to open the door.

Set aside to cool for at least an hour before cutting into 24 squares. Leave to cool completely before serving.

Chocolate chip & hazelnut cookies

In the fight to avoid buying over-sweet biscuits for special occasions or when people are coming for the weekend, these cookies hit the jackpot. They are light, full of flavour and packed with goodness from those delicious hazelnuts (my favourite nut and truly British, although it is an Italian who has made a fortune from the chocolate/hazelnut combo that is Nutella). To keep the cookies light and fluffy, leave until completely cold, then store in airtight plastic boxes: this prevents them from becoming brittle. The unbaked dough also freezes beautifully. Simply bake from frozen at the temperature below for 20 minutes.

Makes
about 27

170g plain flour
1 tsp baking powder
110g unsalted butter, softened
50g granulated sugar
100g light brown soft sugar
½ tsp salt

1 tsp vanilla extract
1 large egg
150g Belgian dark chocolate chips
50g shelled hazelnuts, toasted and
 roughly chopped

Preheat the oven to 180°C/Fan 160°C/Gas 4. Line 3 large baking sheets with baking parchment. (You will have to bake in batches if you don't have this number of sheets or oven shelves.)

Sift the flour and baking powder into a large bowl, then put to one side.

Put the butter and both sugars into another bowl and beat with an electric whisk until light and fluffy. Add the salt, vanilla and egg and beat until well mixed, about 1 minute.

Tip the flour mixure into the butter mixture, along with the chocolate chips and hazelnuts, and beat until combined.

Using 2 teaspoons (1 for scooping and the other for pushing), put rough balls of the dough onto the lined baking sheet, spacing them well apart, as they spread during baking. You'll be able to get 9 on a square baking sheet and about 12 on a rectangular one. Bake for 11–13 minutes, rotating the sheets halfway through, until the cookies are golden around the edges but still soft in the centre.

Set aside to cool on the baking sheets for a couple of minutes. Transfer to a wire rack until completely cold. The cookies will keep in an airtight container for up to 5 days.

Dinosaur cake

My sister Sofie is amazingly talented with sugarcraft and baking. She made this dinosaur cake for her son Charlie, who argued that it was anatomically incorrect, more like a dragon. Whatever, it tastes good and looks good. If you're pressed for time, you can buy two tubs of buttercream rather than making your own.

Serves 20–25 children

250g butter, plus extra for greasing
250g caster sugar
4 large eggs
225g self-raising flour, sifted
½ tsp baking powder
50g cocoa powder
1–2 tbsp milk

FOR THE BUTTERCREAM
325g unsalted butter
300g icing sugar
75g cocoa powder
4 tbsp milk

FOR THE DECORATION
500g green fondant icing
about 100g pink fondant icing, plus tiny
    amounts of white and black fondant icing
icing sugar, for rolling out
1 large bag of big chocolate buttons

Preheat the oven to 190°C/Fan 170°C/Gas 5. Butter two 20cm round cake tins and line with greaseproof paper. Tape two 30cm square cake boards together to make a 60 x 30cm rectangle.

Put the butter and sugar into the bowl of your mixer and cream together. Still mixing, add the eggs, 1 at a time, along with a tablespoon of the flour to avoid curdling. Add the rest of the flour, plus the baking powder, cocoa powder and milk, and fold together until smooth.

Divide the sponge mixture evenly between your prepared tins and bake for 25 minutes. They are ready when a metal skewer inserted in the middle comes out clean.

Leave to cool in the tins, then turn onto a rack and leave until completely cold. Remove the greaseproof paper.

Meanwhile, make the buttercream. Put the butter in a large bowl and use an electric whisk to beat until smooth. Gradually add the icing sugar a large spoonful at a time, beating constantly. Whisk in the cocoa powder with the milk, and continue beating until the mixture is completely smooth. This will be your 'glue'.

CONTINUED OVERLEAF ❯

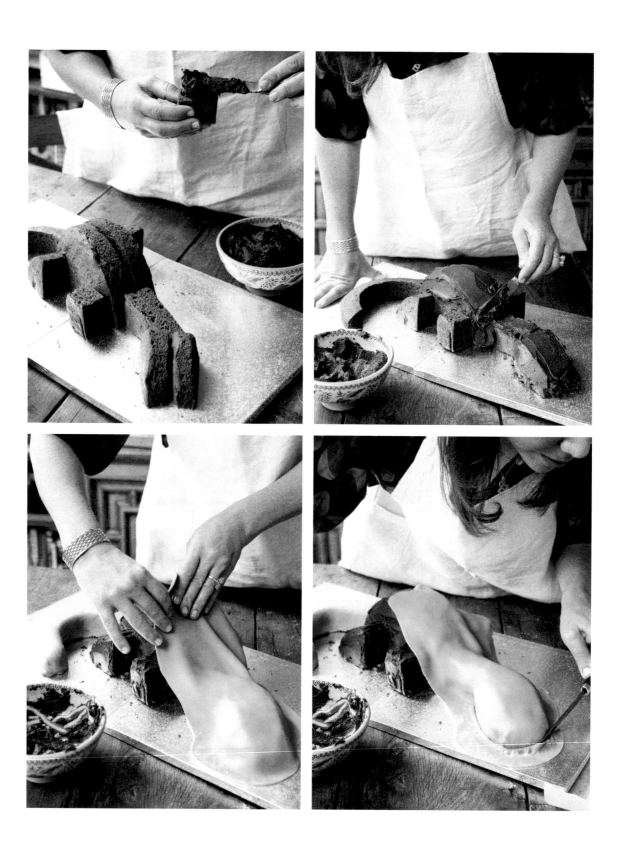

Cut each sponge in half to make 4 half-moons. Spread some buttercream over the flat base of 1 half-moon, then stick the matching half-moon on it to make a humped shape. Spread a little buttercream over the cut edges and stick in the centre of the board. This is the main body of the dinosaur.

To make the tail, take another half-moon of cake and cut a semicircle out of the straight edge, leaving an arch of cake 5cm thick. Spread a little buttercream on 1 cut end of the arched piece, then stick it close to 1 end of the body on the board.

Take the little semicircle of cake you have removed and cut it in half to make 2 curved triangles. These pieces will be the back feet of the dinosaur. Stick them down with buttercream as shown in the photo.

Take the remaining half-moon of cake and cut off a 2cm band along the straight side. Cut this in half. Stick 1 half to the front of the body to make the neck. Cut the other half in 2 and stick these pieces to the sides of the body to make the front legs.

To make the head, take what remains of the final half-moon of cake and cut it in half to make 2 curved triangles. Stick them together with buttercream, then stick onto the neck end of the cake. Carefully cover the whole cake with buttercream.

Cut the green fondant in half and roll out the first piece on a clean work surface dusted with a little icing sugar. It must be big enough to cover the back half of the dinosaur. Lift it on top, carefully smooth down, then trim off any excess fondant. Repeat this step with the remaining green fondant and cover the front half of the body. Use water to make the 2 pieces stick together and smooth out the join.

Roll out the pink fondant and cut out circles of varying sizes to decorate the body. Stick them on with water. Use any leftover trimmings to create toenails, and stick them to the feet.

Roll out a little white fondant and use a small round cutter to stamp out 2 circles for the eyes. Now cut out 8 little triangles for the teeth. Take a little black fondant and roll into 2 small balls for the centre of the eyes. Brush all these pieces with water and stick them onto the head. The teeth go around the lower front of the head, but remember to leave a space for the tongue.

To make the tongue, pinch off a piece of black fondant and roll it into a short 'sausage'. Make a central cut about 2cm into the length, then tease out each side to create a forked tongue. Stick this down with water in the middle of the mouth between the teeth. Lastly, push the chocolate buttons upright into the fondant along the length of the dinosaur's body and tail to mimic spikes.

Survey chaos in the kitchen. Tidy up. Have a glass of wine.

Banana cake

This is a very soft cake that we make a lot. We always have bananas in the fruit bowl, and sometimes can't eat them fast enough, even though we're addicted to Fried Bananas (see page 28). So we use them in this cake. We take the cake with us as travelling fodder, as none of my children will eat any of the food offered on trains or planes: in fact, one of my stepsons used to puke whenever he saw his passport.

The cake is also great served as a pudding. Top it with some cream or crème fraîche, and a fruit purée made by mashing raspberries or strawberries with icing sugar. Try it too as a breakfast bread, add it to a school lunch-box, or offer as a snack when the kids come in starving after swimming or surfing.

The recipe comes from Maravic, who has worked for Ben for many years. She is a great cook, and we worship her spring rolls (see page 188).

Makes
10–12 slices

150g butter, at room temperature
125g light muscovado sugar
225g self-raising flour
4 large ripe bananas (about 550g in
   total, weighed in their skins)

3 medium eggs, beaten
pinch of salt
1 tsp vanilla extract

Preheat the oven to 180°C/Fan 160°C/Gas 4. Line a 21 x 11cm loaf tin with greaseproof paper or a 2lb loaf-tin liner.

Put the butter into a large bowl and whisk until softened. Add the sugar and continue to whisk until the mixture is pale and fluffy. Sift the flour over the top. Mash the bananas in a separate bowl, then add to the flour.

Add the eggs, salt and vanilla and beat until smooth. This is best done with some type of electric whisk.

Spoon the mixture into the prepared tin and bake for 60–80 minutes. The cake is ready when a skewer stuck into the middle comes out clean. Transfer to a wire rack to cool.

Gretchen's bread

When my mother-in-law joins us on holiday, she has been known to come armed with everything needed to make her delicious bread. Although I am competitive in all things, I long ago stopped being troubled by Gretchen's amazing cooking talents. To attempt to outcook her would be futile. I now just try to learn as much as I can. There is something very fundamental and joyous about making your own bread and feeding it to your family. Give it a try.

This is Gretchen's bread recipe, told largely in her own words. I have put in some suggested quantities, relying on the instructions on a packet of strong flour. Note that everything you are working with should be at room temperature.

Makes a
900g loaf

300ml lukewarm water (use a third boiling to the rest cold)
2 tsp clear honey
1 x 7g sachet dried yeast
340g strong white bread flour, preferably organic

160g strong wholemeal bread flour, preferably organic
2 tsp salt
1 tbsp olive oil
1 egg, beaten
up to 150g dryish mashed potato (optional)

'I made bread on holiday because you couldn't buy good bread or even the ingredients on the island. I had two bags of organic strong flour, one white and one brown, and a box of sachets of dried yeast.

'Everything you need to do if you are the sort of cook who likes accurate measurements is on the packet. The people who sell this are anxious that you get it right! They are better than I am on measuring, timing and temperature.

'First put the lukewarm water into a jug. Pour 5 tablespoons of it into a cup and sweeten with half the honey. Add the yeast, then stand the cup in a bowl of quite hot water so that it will not get cold while it's starting to work. This fascinating process involves it gradually coming to life and bubbling up. The yeast is what makes the bread rise.

'Then I get out a large mixing bowl and toss in two-thirds white and one-third brown flour, together with the salt, olive oil and remaining honey, plus an egg. Another magic ingredient you can work in with your hands is an amount of cooked potato.

CONTINUED OVERLEAF ❯

'For the next step, please wear a huge apron and also have oven gloves to hand.

'When the yeast is ready, pour it into the flour and stir it with a big wooden spoon, then start to add the rest of the water. Before it starts to look like dough, put your floury hands in and you can start to get it all together and start kneading it. If you have too much water, you can always add more flour or vice versa.

'Put a dusting of flour and the ball of dough on your surface to finish off the kneading. This is the most enjoyable part, as you find the bread really becoming alive and bouncing back as you push it and turn it.

'Wipe oil around inside the mixing bowl, which you should have left more or less clean. Put your dough back in the big bowl and put that into a large plastic carrier bag to keep it from drying out while it is rising. This is more effective than a cloth. You can leave it for as long as you like. Too long is not a problem. Hurrying the process might be.

'Punch the dough back – it will have risen a lot – and place in a lightly oiled 900g loaf tin. Cover again and leave to prove for about 20 minutes.

'Preheat the oven to 200°C/Fan 180°C/Gas 6.

'Make sure you have heated the oven well before you put the bread in to bake. Treat it gently as you put it in: if you let it jolt, it will be bad.

'Bake for 30–35 minutes. Turn the oven down to 180°C/160°C/Gas 4 and bake for another 15 minutes.

'Over the years another tip a friend gave me is to put a large upturned iron pot over the bread. This should be taken off 10 minutes before the finishing time.

'Try to resist eating the bread until it has cooled right down on a wire rack. It will be more digestible for one thing and go further. The cooked potato makes it last for days.'

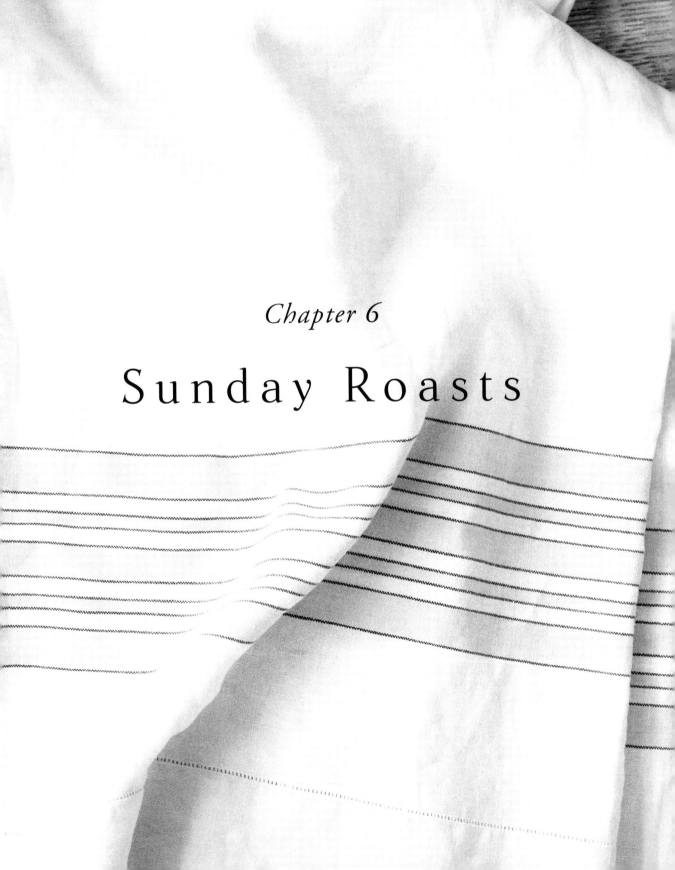

Chapter 6

Sunday Roasts

Most people learn how to cook from their mothers or grandmothers. Although my mother was able to cook brilliantly when she tried, she didn't really enjoy cooking. As a result, my childhood culinary education was somewhat lacking. For instance, we never had roasts other than chicken. When we had roast meat, we struggled to recognise it. One such early encounter has become legendary in my family. We went for lunch with my cousin Laura. When a platter of roast pork was brought to the table, my brother said, 'Oh goodie, chicken.' Everyone laughed and looked a little askance at my mother, as they all knew how little she cooked.

I love roast meat of all kinds. We tend to have roasts in the colder months, as the rest of the time Ben will be outside barbecuing on the Big Green Egg (he is not so keen on patio cooking when the temperature drops below 5°C). The Aga is good for roasting, though the roasting oven is much hotter than a conventional oven – probably 240°C/Fan 220°C/Gas 9 – so that is where I brown and crisp joints briefly before moving them to another of the ovens for slower cooking. Roast potatoes cook beautifully on the floor of the roasting oven, and I also cook bacon in there.

My favourite roast meat perhaps is beef, and the recipe I give here for a roast rib (see page 162) works every time, producing perfect pink slices – accompanied by the best Yorkshire puddings in the world (see page 166)! I would serve it with some horseradish-flavoured mashed potato (add 1–3 tablespoons creamed horseradish to 1kg potatoes mashed with cream, milk and butter, tasting after each spoonful as horseradish can be very hot).

In Devon we roast a lot of lamb, which we buy in bulk from the local butcher and keep in the freezer. Occasionally, we have roast pork, as we are all very keen on crackling. We also love the apple sauce that traditionally accompanies it. Devon used to be the cider capital of England, so every farm would have its apple orchard. Nowadays the number of orchards has diminished, sadly, and you might see only a few remnant trees in a garden somewhere, or be reminded by the name of a street in a new-build estate (Apple Way or Orchard Street). We have a few trees at Grange, both eating and cooking apples, which we do pick and use.

Of course, you must never forget about the wonderful accompaniments that are traditionally served with roast joints. There are a few potato suggestions in this chapter, but you will also find vegetable ideas in Chapters 4 and 6. A good gravy is vital as well – the one with the roast beef is spectacular – but you can make a simple one using some flour, the roast juices and some stock (fine from a stock cube).

Of course, there is no compulsion to have traditional dishes with roast meat. I often serve Indian-style vegetables, taking inspiration from Meera Sodha's *Made in India* and *Fresh India*. This also means vegetarians are properly catered for and don't just get a baked potato as an afterthought. Salads too are lovely with roasts in the summer, and cold meat leftovers come in very useful for picnics or packed lunches.

Roast rib of beef with a mustard crust

This beef has been a winner in our family ever since James Mackenzie – of the Pipe & Glass Inn in East Yorkshire – cooked it for one of my TV series. He was also the one who famously taught me to cook the accompanying Yorkshire puddings (see page 166). I have roasted this beef for Sunday lunch, and occasionally for Christmas Day lunch. It is an expensive cut, so you don't want it to go wrong, and with this recipe, it won't. I love the 'trellis' of vegetables keeping the meat above the surface of the pan and allowing air to flow around the joint. It's a game-changer because the vegetables add enormous flavour to the rich gravy as well.

Serves 8–10

2.5–2.6kg forerib of beef (about 2 ribs)
rapeseed oil
2 carrots, washed and roughly chopped
1 onion, peeled and roughly chopped
1 leek, washed and roughly chopped
1 celery stick, washed and roughly chopped
2 tbsp English mustard paste
3 tbsp Dijon mustard
2 tbsp wholegrain mustard

FOR THE MULLED WINE GRAVY
rapeseed oil, for frying
2 large onions, peeled and sliced
500ml homemade mulled wine or red wine
red wine vinegar (optional)
2 tbsp plain flour
1 litre beef stock (a stock cube is fine)
2 tbsp redcurrant jelly
salt and freshly ground black pepper

Preheat the oven to 220°C/Fan 200°C/Gas 7. Put a roasting tray inside to heat up.

Sear the joint in the hot roasting tray on top of the stove, using a little of the oil, until golden brown all over. Transfer the beef to a plate.

Make a criss-cross arrangement of the vegetables in the roasting tray – this 'trellis' will serve as a rack for the meat.

Mix the three different types of mustard in a bowl and rub all over the meat. Cover the exposed bones with foil

Place the beef on the vegetables, cover the whole tray with foil and roast for 20 minutes. Remove the foil, reduce the temperature to 180°C/Fan 160°C/Gas 4 and continue roasting for a further 1½ hours (the meat will be medium rare).

CONTINUED OVERLEAF ❯

Meanwhile, start the gravy. Put a little rapeseed oil in a large saucepan and fry the onions over a medium heat until soft and caramelised (about 20–30 minutes). Add the mulled wine and bring to the boil over a high heat. Taste and if you find it too sweet, add a touch of red wine vinegar. Lower the heat and simmer for another 30 minutes.

When the meat is ready, remove it from the tray and leave it to rest, covered loosely with foil, for at least 20 minutes.

Pour the excess fat out of the roasting tray, but keep the roasted veg in it. Place the tray over the heat, add the flour and cook, stirring for 2 minutes. Pour in the beef stock and stir well, scraping up any crusty bits from the tray. Bring to the boil and simmer for 3–4 minutes. It should thicken up a little. Strain through a sieve into the pan of cooked onion and mulled wine, using the back of a spoon to get out as much flavour as possible out of the vegetables.

Stir the redcurrant jelly into the oniony gravy and check the seasoning.

Carve the meat and serve with Crushed Roast Potatoes (see page 225), a simple green veg and the delicious gravy.

Perfect Yorkshire puddings

My mother was brought up partly in Yorkshire, but somehow the Yorkshire pudding passed her by. I'm not sure when I first had one, but it wasn't at home, I know that for sure. It never occurred to me to make one until I met James Mackenzie, who came on the first ever Christmas show. Chefs like him can work magic, but can we really achieve the same miracles at home? Yes, absolutely, and I'm not sure a week has gone by since that I haven't made Yorkshire puddings. Please believe me when I say this recipe has never failed me. The only problem is that you make them, put them on the table, turn your back for two minutes and that's it, you've missed your chance.

Please note, Yorkshire puddings aren't just for Sundays or roast dinners; they rock as a snack for ravenous teens.

Makes 12

3 large eggs
150ml full-fat milk
130g plain flour
goose or duck fat, or beef dripping
salt and freshly ground white pepper

Preheat the oven to 220°C/Fan 200°C/Gas 7. Set out a 12-hole bun tin.

Place the eggs and milk in a mixing bowl and whisk together. Sift in the flour and mix with a hand blender until you've got a smooth batter. Leave to stand for 10 minutes, then transfer to a jug, which will make it easier to pour into the tin.

Place a tablespoon of fat in each hole of the bun tin. Put in the oven for a couple of minutes, until smoking hot.

Season the batter immediately before you pour it into the smoking hot tin; this will stop the salt breaking down the egg and your puddings will rise really well.

Fill each hole until nearly full. Bake for 15 minutes, until puffed up and golden, then eat hot and enjoy.

Roast belly of pork

Every time I have roast pork, I think of the Laura Ingalls Wilder books, which include *Little House on the Prairie*. I read them as a child, and have re-read them as an adult, and I find the depiction of settler life so evocative. The description of Laura's first taste of pork crackling has remained with me to this day, and I too have never forgotten the same experience. The crackling in this recipe, borrowed from Hugh Fearnley-Whittingstall's *River Cottage Meat Book*, is brilliant. Serve the meat with Crushed Roast Potatoes and Apple Sauce (see pages 225 and 170).

Serves 8

thick end of pork belly, about 6 ribs
fresh thyme leaves
salt and freshly ground black pepper

Preheat the oven to 220°C/Fan 200°C/Gas 7.

Place the belly in a roasting tray, skin-side up, and dry it with kitchen paper if slightly damp. Score the skin with a sharp knife, making the cuts as close together as you can manage, and rub with thyme, salt and pepper.

Place in the hot oven and roast for 30 minutes, then turn the temperature down to 180°C/Fan 160°C/Gas 4. Continue roasting the pork for another hour, or until the skin has crackled, and the juices run clear when the meat is pierced by a skewer. If the crackling isn't crackly enough, put the oven up again and leave for a few minutes.

When ready to serve, cut the crackling off the pork and break it into pieces. Carve the meat into thick slices. Put a couple of slices of meat on each plate with a bit of crackling and a dollop of our wonderful apple sauce (see overleaf).

Grange apple sauce

There are quite a few apple trees in the garden at Grange. The eating apples are sent to a local press up the hill, and I use the juice in cocktails and tea (see Chapter 10), and of course the kids drink it by the gallon. The cookers we purée into apple sauce, which is great with pork or oily fish like mackerel, and for making apple crumble and apple yoghurt, for serving with meringues and cream, for flavouring pork sandwiches – you name it, we've done it at some time.

Serves 6

2 cooking apples, peeled, cored and sliced
20g soft brown sugar
20g butter
2 cloves (optional)
75ml water

Put all the ingredients into a suitable pan and cover with a lid. Put over a low heat and cook for about 10–15 minutes, stirring occasionally. The apples will soften into a purée. Add a splash more water if the purée seems very thick.

Carefully pick out the cloves, then mash the apple with a potato masher to get rid of any remaining lumps. Cool, then chill until needed. To serve, spoon into a serving dish.

Roast lamb

It was Ben's idea to get the rare-breed sheep that we have in Devon. They are comical creatures, and I find it difficult to think of eating them. However, if we didn't, they'd take over the entire garden.

I tend to cook lamb in the slow-cooker (see page 80), but Ben likes to roast it more conventionally. Our bible so far as meat is concerned is *The River Cottage Meat Book* by Hugh Fearnley-Whittingstall, and the recipe below is based on his. Hugh includes anchovies, spiked into the meat along with the garlic and rosemary, but Ben prefers it without them.

Serves 4–6

1 x 2kg leg or shoulder of lamb or mutton
2 large garlic cloves, peeled and cut into slivers
2 sprigs of fresh rosemary, divided into smaller pieces

olive oil
125ml dry white wine
100ml water
plain flour (optional)
salt and freshly ground black pepper

Preheat the oven to 230°C/Fan 210°C/Gas 8.

Put the lamb in a suitably sized roasting tin. Using a small, sharp knife, make little slits about 2–3cm deep all over the top. Into each of these slits push a sliver of garlic and a few rosemary leaves.

Rub a little olive oil all over the surface, then season well with salt and pepper. Roast for 30 minutes. Remove from the oven and pour over the wine. Lower the temperature to 170°C/Fan 150°C/Gas 3, and cook the lamb for a further 1–1½ hours, depending on how pink you like it.

Around 15 minutes or so before the lamb is ready, pour the water into the tray and stir it around. When the meat is done to your liking, remove it from the tin and leave to rest in a warm place for at least 20 minutes.

Make a gravy to your taste, adding some flour if you like, or simply adding a little more wine to the juices already in the tray. Hugh suggests adding a little redcurrant jelly, which we also do to the beef gravy on page 162.

Carve and serve with the juices or gravy, some roast potatoes and a simple green veg. And you must have some mint sauce or redcurrant jelly.

Roast chicken

This roast chicken comes from William Miller, husband of my great friend, Trine. Both of them are very good cooks, as well as being life enhancers, and we two families meet and eat often. The recipe is largely in William's own words, with slight additions and amendments from me. I would serve the chicken with his Crushed Roast Potatoes (see page 178).

Serves 6

1 x 1.5kg free-range chicken
good olive oil
1 lemon
2–4 garlic cloves, peeled and bashed a bit, or 1 onion, peeled and halved
2 tsp dried tarragon
20g butter
Maldon sea salt and freshly ground black pepper

FOR THE GRAVY
1 tbsp plain flour
1 chicken stock cube
about 450ml boiling water (perhaps from the vegetable cooking)
1–2 tbsp alcohol (red wine, Marsala or sherry are all good)

'Preheat the oven to 200°C/Fan 180°C/Gas 6. Remove all the paraphernalia that so often comes with a shop-bought chicken – elastic bands, bags of offal, etc. Smother the chicken with good olive oil and squeeze a lemon over the whole body, shoving the remains of the lemon inside the cavity along with the semi-crushed garlic cloves. Sprinkle the salt liberally over the chicken. This really helps to dry the skin while cooking and makes it wonderfully crisp and tasty: crispy skin is the secret of a great roast chicken! On top of the salt sprinkle a good amount of dried tarragon (dried seems to have more flavour than fresh). Place several large knobs of butter along the top of the chicken, which will melt over it as it starts to cook. Add a glass of water to the tin – this helps to stop the juices and fat from burning on the bottom and creates the base juices for the gravy.

'Calculate the cooking time at 20 minutes per 450g, plus 20 minutes. For a 1.5kg chicken this works out to about 1¼ hours. Put the chicken into the oven and roast for 20 minutes, then lower the temperature to 190°C/Fan 170°C/Gas 5 and continue to roast for the remaining time, until the skin is really brown and crisp. Don't take it out if the skin still looks pale, as it will probably be raw in the middle and just won't taste as good. If you are worried about fat spitting over the inside of your oven so it smokes forever after, cover the bird in foil for the first 45 minutes and take it off for the last 30 minutes or so to let the direct heat crisp up the skin.

CONTINUED OVERLEAF ❯

'Check the chicken is cooked by pushing a skewer into the thigh to see if the juices run clear. If not, continue to roast and check at 5-minute intervals. Lift the chicken with the opening pointing downwards and drain the juices from the inside into the roasting tray. Move the chicken onto a warm serving plate, cover in foil and stand for 10–15 minutes.

'Meanwhile, for the gravy, drain all the juices into a clear heatproof jug, leaving about 2 tablespoons in the tray. Set the jug aside for a while and the liquid will separate into the dark juices and fat. Once this has happened, drain away the fat. Place the roasting tray over a low heat and sprinkle in the flour. Using a spatula or flat-ended wooden spoon, stir the juices into the flour, gently scraping up the fat and residue in the bottom of the tray to mix everything together. (This will make life a lot easier too when you come to wash the tray!) Crumble in the stock cube and stir gently, breaking up any lumps, then slowly add the boiling water and stir well as it thickens in the heat. When it has started to thicken properly, thin a little with alcohol to add flavour. Add the jug of reserved juices and simmer for another 10 minutes to cook off the alcohol and slightly thicken the gravy some more.'

William's crushed roast potatoes

There is heated debate in my family about how to do roast potatoes, so much so that one Christmas we had both my sister Sofie's and my brother Henry's versions. Therefore, this recipe comes from outside the family, although barely, as we spend so much time with William Miller and his wife Trine. William is the best meat-carver I have ever seen – on account of being the son of two doctors, he claims! These potatoes, which he says are perhaps closer to chips, go with everything, but are particularly good with Trine's Salsa Verde (see page 56).

Serves 4–6

750g small new potatoes
sea salt flakes
olive oil or (if you have it) goose fat
fresh rosemary or thyme
anchovies (optional)

Preheat the oven to 200°C/Fan 180°C/Gas 6.

Boil the potatoes until soft, about 10–12 minutes, depending on size.

Drain and place on a large, flat baking tray and crush lightly with the back of a spatula or wooden spoon so that each potato cracks open. (Do not squash completely flat – this is not mashed potatoes.)

Sprinkle liberal amounts of sea salt over the potatoes, and then plenty of olive oil or goose fat. Add a sprinkling of fresh rosemary or thyme, and the anchovies if you like them (they're a good addition), then roast for 20 minutes, or until crisp and brown.

Baked fish

We have stayed a couple of times on the Moroccan coast at a beautiful house owned by some friends, and I have relished every minute. In one sense it's a kids' holiday, as the boys go surfing all the time, but for me it is a culinary holiday because the food is unbelievably good. There are fresh salads, vegetables and fruit from the garden, Moroccan pastries, chicken tagines, and fish that leap straight out of the Atlantic onto the barbecue. It's no wonder I never risked having a lie-in – I was far too frightened I would miss breakfast!

Serves 4–6

900g new potatoes, halved if large
2 tbsp olive oil
750g red, yellow or orange tomatoes, sliced in half if large
1–2 heads of garlic
2 lemons
2 x 900g whole fish, such as bream, cleaned and scaled
small bag of rocket

salt and freshly ground black pepper

FOR THE DRESSING
30g parsley
30g walnuts
20g Parmesan cheese, freshly grated
5–6 tbsp olive oil
1–2 tbsp red wine vinegar

Preheat the oven to 200°C/Fan 180°C/Gas 6. Meanwhile, bring a large pan of water to the boil. Add the new potatoes, along with a good pinch of salt, half-cover with a lid and simmer for 10 minutes. Drain, then return the potatoes to the pan and add the oil. Season well.

Spoon the potatoes into a large roasting tin, or two small ones if necessary. Scatter the tomatoes around them. Cut the top off each head of garlic and cut the lemons in half. Tuck them around the potatoes. Drizzle any oil remaining in the saucepan over the garlic and tomatoes. Season again.

Nestle the fish in amongst the potatoes and tomatoes, season everything again and roast in the oven for 40 minutes. The fish is ready when you can easily pull the spine away from the flesh.

While the fish is in the oven, blitz all the dressing ingredients in a blender and season well. If you prefer a coarser texture, finely chop the parsley and walnuts by hand, then mix in a bowl with the Parmesan, oil and vinegar. To serve, place a portion of fish on each plate, add a few potatoes, tomatoes and garlic cloves, a roasted lemon half and drizzle with the dressing.

Potato bake with anchovies

This is a famous Swedish dish shown to me by my friend Anna. In Sweden it is known as *Janssons frestelse*, or 'Jansson's temptation'. It is indeed very tempting – baked creamy potatoes with the salty hit of anchovies (originally, sprats were used). Anna says she sometimes uses oil from the anchovy tin in the cooking, and tends not to add salt as the anchovies are already so salty. The dish can be made in advance and reheated, but Anna tends to make it fresh. It is great as an accompaniment to a grilled chop or steak, or a roast joint of meat.

Serves 4

6 medium waxy or baking potatoes, peeled
3 medium white onions, peeled
10 tinned anchovies, or more if you like
butter, for frying and dotting
300ml double cream
50g fresh breadcrumbs

Preheat the oven to 200°C/Fan 180°C/Gas 6.

Cut the potatoes into slices, then into matchsticks. Put in a pan of cold water to prevent browning and to get rid of excess starch.

Slice the onions very thinly. Heat a knob of butter in a large frying pan and sweat the onions, stirring occasionally, until they are golden and transparent.

Butter a large ovenproof dish. Put in one layer of potato – use a third – then a layer of half the onion. Add 5 of the anchovies, spreading them out evenly, then a few small knobs of butter. Repeat these layers, finishing with a final layer of potato sticks. Pour the cream over and scatter with the breadcrumbs. Putting some more butter on top will make the crumbs even crisper.

Bake for 40 minutes, or a little bit longer in the hot oven of an Aga. The dish is ready when the potatoes are soft when pierced with a knife and the top is nicely brown and crisp.

Chapter 7

Picnics & Barbecues

It is a real passion for us, eating outside. For me, I think it probably stemmed from when I was a little girl, living near Hungerford in Berkshire. Whenever we drove across the common on our way home, I would see people with foldaway chairs and tables picnicking next to their cars at the side of the road, and I longed to do the same. This mystified my poor parents, who just couldn't see the appeal.

Ben also loves cooking outside, and is inseparable most of the year from one of his barbecues. At Grange we have a Big Green Egg, but for picnics on the beach we take a cheap and cheerful bucket barbecue. In the winter we often go to a Devon hut that we call The Belvedere because it has magnificent views, and there we cook on the big grate at the foot of the stone chimney.

We normally have a selection of warm foods, cold foods, and meat, fish or veg to be cooked on the barbecue. Ben is always in charge: he goes to the butcher or fishmonger and often comes back with a selection of burgers, kebabs, steaks, spare ribs and sausages, plus whole fish that vary in size from sardine to bass. Once he came back with rabbit burgers, which were divine and went down a storm with everyone, but we couldn't breathe a word to the children!

I make things like a quiche or sausage or spring rolls at home and take them with me mainly because I don't want people to be starving and grumpy while waiting for the hot food to be served. I also take boxes of salad ingredients, jars of dressing, seasonings, sauces and marinades, plus lots of kitchen paper.

If I have chosen to take a warm stew-type dish, I transport it in my antique Norwegian container, which has double walls, like a vacuum flask. You put the hot food in the middle container, put the lid on, then close the whole thing up. It keeps food hot for hours, but is very heavy and needs two people to carry it. There are many modern versions now, but if don't have one, simply put hot food in a dish with a lid, wrap it in foil, then put it in a cool box lined with double foil and top with hot bags (rather than ice blocks) or a hot-water bottle. For carbohydrate accompaniment I take some uncooked couscous in a bowl, along with a Thermos flask of boiling water, and prepare it once everything else is nearly ready to serve.

At the beach, Ben balances the bucket barbecue on stones, then all the men stand around him. There is nothing we women can do about this; it's writ in their DNA for fire to be male territory. Only later, when the flames have died down and the men are eating, can the children approach with their skewers and cook their marshmallows. On one occasion at The Belvedere, the children got on the roof and weed down the chimney. Their snorts of laughter alerted us. After a while they came down and asked if they could do their marshmallows now. Well, no, we said, the fire is out because of you. As someone remarked, it was the ultimate definition of raining on your own parade.

Maravic's spring rolls

Maravic, who has worked for Ben for many years, was born in the Philippines, and I am now determined to visit this beautiful, complex country. For many years, whenever we have had any gatherings in London – from children's parties to my father-in-law Viv's wake – Maravic has brought round a huge pile of her spring rolls. There are never any left over because they are delicious hot or cold: I have eaten them at all times of the day and night. We used to dip them in a shop-bought chilli sauce, but now I use home-made chilli chutney (see page 204) as a dipping sauce and have been amazed at the difference.

These spring rolls freeze beautifully (see tip overleaf), so it's worth making a big batch and freezing some for next time. Maravic says we should feel free to use seasonal veg – red cabbage, leeks, celeriac – as well as the carrots and celery.

Makes 50

70g dried fine glass noodles
1 large onion, peeled
2 large carrots, scrubbed
1 large courgette, trimmed
2 celery sticks, trimmed
100g fine green beans, trimmed
¼ white cabbage
1 large garlic clove, peeled

sunflower oil
250g skinless, boneless chicken breast
    or thigh, finely sliced
large handful of beansprouts
soy sauce, to taste
50 spring roll wrappers, about 12.5cm
    in diameter
salt and freshly ground black pepper

Put the noodles into a medium bowl. Cover with boiling water and set aside to soak while you make the filling.

Prepare your vegetables. Chop the onion finely. Then, using the large holes on a box grater, grate the carrots and courgette. Finely slice the celery, green beans and cabbage into strips. Crush the garlic.

Heat 2 tablespoons oil in a large frying pan and lightly fry the onion over a medium heat until golden brown. Add the chicken and cook for a few minutes, until it has turned white.

Add the carrots, celery, green beans, cabbage and garlic to the pan. Season to taste with salt and pepper and continue to stir-fry for about 5 minutes, chopping the chicken into smaller pieces with the edge of the spoon.

CONTINUED OVERLEAF ❯

Drain the noodles well, add to the pan along with the beansprouts and stir-fry for a further 2 minutes on a high heat. Add a splash of soy sauce, to taste. Spoon the contents of the pan into a large bowl and allow to cool.

Separate 2 or 3 spring roll wrappers at a time and lay them out on a board with corner points at top and bottom, like a diamond. Scoop a heaped tablespoon of the noodle mixture onto each wrapper just below the centre. Lift up the bottom corner and place it over the filling, then roll up the rest of the wrapper, tucking in the sides as you go. Brush the loose end of each wrapper with water and stick it down. Transfer the rolls to a separate board, then continue making more rolls until all the wrappers and filling have been used up.

Heat a 2cm depth of vegetable oil in a shallow frying pan. When hot, cook a few rolls at a time, until golden brown, turning them over halfway through.

⟩ TIPS ⟨

To make the rolls that little bit healthier, you can bake rather than fry them. Preheat the oven to 200°C/Fan 180°C/Gas 6. Brush each roll with oil (I sometimes use a mixture of sunflower and sesame oil), then place on baking sheets and bake for 15–20 minutes, turning the sheets as necesssary. They're not quite as crispy, but still very more-ish.

If you want to freeze a batch of uncooked rolls for future use, simply spread them out on a parchment-lined tray and freeze until hard. Transfer to a lidded plastic container and freeze for up to a month. To bake from frozen, preheat the oven as above, brush the rolls with oil and bake for about 20 minutes on a baking sheet, until golden and hot right through.

Homemade beef burgers

Many people feel it's a bit of chore to make their own burgers or fish fingers, but I like to because it's the only way I can be sure what has gone into them. Ben sometimes buys ready-made burgers when we are in Devon, but I can't complain too much, as he is the one who does the shopping, and he gets them from an excellent local butcher.

These burgers are perfect for picnics or barbecues at home and away – and, even better, the boys all like them!

Makes 6

1 medium onion, peeled
1 garlic clove, peeled
500g good-quality beef mince
1 tsp Dijon mustard
1 tsp Worcestershire sauce
1 tsp soy sauce
1 large egg
pinch of chilli power (optional)
plain flour, for coating (optional)

olive or sunflower oil, for frying
salt and freshly ground black pepper

TO SERVE
6 good-quality burger buns
selection of toppings, e.g. sliced Cheddar,
    lettuce, tomatoes, gherkins, mustard,
    mayo, ketchup

Chop the onion roughly, then put it in a blender with the garlic and blend to a purée. Decant into a large bowl.

Add all the remaining burger ingredients, apart from the flour and oil, and mix until the texture is like sausage meat.

Divide into six equal pieces, roll into balls and flatten to the size of the burger buns. Coat each burger in a fine dusting of flour if you like. If you have time, put the burgers on a plate and chill for 20 minutes or so; this helps them firm up.

Heat 1 tablespoon oil in a frying pan and fry the burgers for 2–3 minutes on each side, according to how rare or well done you like them. You could of course cook them on a hot barbecue or griddle pan, in which case simply brush them first with oil. Use a spatula to lightly press them down, making sure they are in full contact with the hot pan or rack.

Lightly toast the buns and put a burger in the middle. Serve with all the toppings laid out so that people can help themselves.

Picnic quiche

I was inspired to learn how to make quiches by those I tasted at Sally Clarke's deli in Kensington. A classic quiche, from Lorraine, is a pastry case containing a custard of eggs and cream, with added onion, bacon and cheese. (I have made the cheese optional here, as the cream filling is very rich.) Once you have mastered the basic custard recipe, you can ring the changes by using fish and different vegetables – smoked haddock would be good, perhaps with some onion and red pepper; fried sliced mushrooms are also a tasty addition.

Quiches are very useful, especially when you are organising a picnic. Wrap the cold quiche in clingfilm, preferably still in its tin, and transport like that. Cut into wedges when you are at your destination.

If you don't want to make your own shortcrust pastry, use 275g ready-made.

Serves 10–12

2 tbsp olive oil
2 medium onions, peeled and finely
    chopped
450g bacon pieces or ready-chopped
    pancetta
100g Gruyère cheese, grated (optional)

FOR THE SHORTCRUST PASTRY
180g plain flour, plus a little extra for
    dusting

90g cold butter, chopped
3–4 tbsp iced water (just add ice to
    a small glass of water)
salt and freshly ground black pepper

FOR THE CUSTARD
2 large eggs, plus 1 medium egg yolk
300ml double cream
freshly grated nutmeg

First make the pastry. Put the flour, butter and a pinch of salt in a food processor and whizz until the mixture looks like fine sand. Add the iced water and pulse until the mixture starts to form a dough. Tip into a bowl and very quickly knead it with your hands until it comes together and looks smooth. Flatten into a disc and wrap in clingfilm. Chill in the freezer for 10 minutes. Don't forget it, or it will harden into an unrollable slab!

Dust a clean work surface with a little flour and roll out the pastry quickly and evenly. Use it to line a 23 x 4cm loose-bottomed fluted tart tin. Trim the edges, then prick the base all over. Place in the freezer for about 20 minutes, until firm.

CONTINUED OVERLEAF ❯

Meanwhile, preheat the oven to 200°C/Fan 180°C/Gas 6.

Line the pastry case with baking parchment and baking beans, place it on a baking sheet and blind-bake for 15 minutes. Remove the parchment and beans, and return the pastry case to the oven for a further 5–10 minutes, until the base feels and looks dry. Turn off the oven and remove the tin, leaving it on the baking sheet.

To make the filling, heat the oil in a medium pan, then stir in the onions and a good pinch of salt. Cook for 2–3 minutes. Take a sheet of baking parchment, scrunch it up and wet it well. Open it out slightly and place on top of the onions. Cover the pan with a lid and turn the heat down to very low. Cook for about 25 minutes, until the onions have softened. Check them every 8–10 minutes and give them a stir, replacing the parchment and lid every time. If they start to brown and look as if they'll burn, add a good splash of water. They need to be really soft once they're done: if you don't cook them for long enough, they'll be hard and crunchy when you bite into the quiche, plus there's a chance they'll curdle the cream. Leave to cool.

Meanwhile, cook the bacon pieces or pancetta in a large frying pan until golden and just starting to crisp. (If your pan is not big enough, you'll need to do this in two batches.) Extra oil shouldn't be necessary, but add a drizzle if you think it is. Remove from the pan with a slotted spoon and drain on kitchen paper. Leave to cool.

Preheat the oven to 150°C/Fan 130°C/Gas 2.

Spoon the onion into the base of the pastry case and spread it out. Do the same with the bacon, spreading the bits evenly over the top. Whisk together the eggs, egg yolk and double cream in a jug, then season with salt, pepper and nutmeg. Carefully pour this mixture into the pastry case. If using the grated cheese, mix it into the jug of eggs, or sprinkle it over the filled quiche.

Return to the oven, still on the baking sheet, and bake for around 40 minutes, rotating the tin halfway through so it cooks evenly. The top should have just a slight wobble. Serve warm or cold.

Sausage rolls

I have been making my own sausage rolls for quite a while now, using a Jamie Oliver recipe as a starting point and making my own tweaks. They're perfect for picnics and parties, even for canapés (if small enough). Sprinkle with sesame seeds for extra crunch, and offer some chutney for dipping (see page 204).

Makes 20–30, depending on size

1 x 375g packet ready-rolled all-butter puff pastry
plain flour, for dusting
1 medium egg
splash of milk

FOR THE FILLING
about 2 tbsp olive oil
1 medium onion, peeled and finely sliced
6 good-quality pork, beef or lamb sausages
2 tbsp chopped parsley
handful of fresh breadcrumbs
freshly grated nutmeg
salt and freshly ground black pepper

Preheat the oven to 180°C/Fan 160°C/Gas 4. Have ready a large baking tray.

To make the filling, heat the olive oil in pan and add the onion. Cook gently for about 20 minutes, until soft and golden. Spread out on a plate to cool. Using a sharp knife, slit the skin of the sausages and pop the meat out. Put it in a mixing bowl with the cooled onion, the parsley and the breadcrumbs. Add a good grating of nutmeg, plus salt and pepper to taste, then mix well with your clean hands.

Unroll the puff pastry on a lightly floured work surface, with the longer side nearest you. Cut it in half from left to right into 2 equal rectangles. Halve the sausagemeat mixture and roll each half into a sausage as long as the pastry. Place a sausage along the centre of each rectangle.

Mix the egg and milk together, then brush it around the edges of the pastry. Fold one side of the pastry over so that the edges meet and enclose the filling inside. Press your fingers or the end of a spoon around the edges to seal well.

Cut each long roll into 10 or 15 pieces, depending what size you want, and space them out on the baking tray. (They could also be frozen at this stage for at least a month. To cook from frozen, just add 10 minutes to the cooking time below.)

Brush the rolls with the rest of the egg wash and bake for 20–25 minutes, turning the tray halfway through, until golden and the filling is completely cooked.

Barbecued spare ribs

In the United States, spare ribs are barbecued plain, then served with a sweet and sticky sauce. You can do the same, but often it's much easier to cook them in the oven, either sitting in or brushed with the sauce, then take them with you to your picnic spot. They could be given a quick warm-through on the barbecue if you like. You can flavour the ribs with an American or Oriental marinade/sauce. I've given a couple of recipes below, and you should choose only one of them!

Spare ribs always make me think of David Beckham. Odd, I know, but it will become clear… I went once to see Bay play football at Wormwood Scrubs, where a load of different schools were playing that day. When I arrived, Bay was thrilled to bits. He had gone to say hello to a really sweet dog, and the person at the other end of the lead happened to be David Beckham (there to watch one of his sons playing). Bay's team also won their match, so later on I said, 'What a red-letter day!' and (still in awe) he said, 'Mum, you have no idea.'

We had spare ribs that evening, and because his friend Vincent didn't want his, Bay had two helpings, followed by pumpkin pie, his favourite. To sum up, it was literally the best day of his life because he got to meet David Beckham, he played in a match that his team won, he had two helpings of spare ribs, and finished off with his favourite pudding … what more could a boy want?

Serves 4–6

1.5kg pork spare ribs
salt and freshly ground black pepper

FOR THE AMERICAN MARINADE/SAUCE
1 tbsp vegetable oil
½ onion, peeled and finely chopped
1 garlic clove, peeled and finely chopped
6 tbsp tomato ketchup
2 tsp English mustard powder
3 tbsp Worcestershire sauce
2 tbsp wine vinegar

3 tbsp clear honey (in the US they would
   use maple syrup)
Tabasco sauce, to taste

FOR THE CHINESE-STYLE MARINADE/SAUCE
2 tsp five-spice powder
2 tsp ground star anise, or 1 whole star
   anise, crushed
6 tbsp soy sauce
6 tbsp clear honey
4 tbsp hoisin sauce
4 tbsp tomato purée

Put the spare ribs into a large saucepan, cover with boiling water, add a little salt, and leave to simmer for about 25 minutes. This softens the flesh more efficiently than simply baking. Drain the ribs well and leave to cool completely.

If making the American marinade, heat the oil in a pan, add the onion and garlic and cook for 5–10 minutes. Add the remaining ingredients and simmer for a further 3 minutes. Set aside to cool.

If making the Chinese-style marinade, simply mix all the ingredients together in a bowl.

Pour your chosen marinade over the spare ribs, mix them around a bit to coat thoroughly, and leave to marinate for 1–4 hours.

Preheat the oven to 200°C/Fan 180°C/Gas 6, or preheat a barbecue or griddle pan.

Remove the ribs from the marinade and lay out on a baking sheet. Season with salt and pepper. Place in the oven and roast for 10 minutes. Brush with the marinade and return to the oven for another 10 minutes. Brush again with the marinade and roast for a final 10 minutes. Cool a little before eating. You'll need lots of kitchen paper.

Marinades

There are two reasons for marinating meat, fish or vegetables that are to be grilled or barbecued: to contribute flavour and to prevent dryness. The usual ingredients included in marinades are oil for lubrication, along with wine, vinegar, citrus juices or yoghurt for flavour, which can be further enhanced by the addition of herbs and/or spices.

Marinate your meat for up to eight hours, or overnight; chicken for two or three hours; and fish for up to one hour. Use a large bowl or a sealable heavy-duty freezer bag, and store in the fridge. Do not add salt to any marinade, as it draws out moisture from meat or fish.

Each marinade serves 4–6

Yoghurt marinade

You can flavour yoghurt in many different ways. Try tarragon or sage with chicken, mint or rosemary with lamb, sage or thyme with pork, etc. Alternatively, add spices, such as ground cumin, coriander and curry powder, for an Indian flavour.

2 tbsp olive oil
150ml plain yoghurt
2 garlic cloves, peeled and crushed
2 tbsp finely choppped herbs or 1 tbsp spice/spice mix
1 tsp freshly ground black pepper

Oriental marinade

Good with poultry, fish or prawns.

4 tbsp sunflower oil
4 tbsp dry sherry
1 tbsp soy sauce
2 garlic cloves, peeled and crushed
½ tsp freshly ground black pepper

Steak marinade

This makes steak – whether sirloin, rump, rib eye or fillet – taste really wonderful. We use it mostly when barbecuing.

2 tbsp olive oil
2 tbsp soy sauce
2 tbsp balsamic vinegar
1 tbsp maple syrup
sliced fresh chilli, to taste
sliced garlic, to taste
salt and freshly ground black pepper

Herb marinade

Use this for meat, fish, poultry or vegetables.

4 tbsp olive oil
2 tbsp wine (red or white), vinegar or lemon juice
1 garlic clove, peeled and crushed
2 tbsp finely chopped mixed herbs (parsley, dill, tarragon, basil, thyme, mint, according to taste really)
½ tsp freshly ground black pepper

The method for all the marinades opposite is very similar: mix the ingredients together in a large shallow dish, then immerse the food in the marinade for the required time. If you prefer, the Oriental, Herb and Steak marinades could simply be brushed onto the food before and during cooking. Note that the Yoghurt Marinade should be brushed off *before* cooking.

Asian tomato & chilli chutney

This recipe is one of many that have in some way come from my friend Eloise, who has been a huge influence on my cooking. She is extraordinarily talented as a chef, but her use of colour brings an extra something to what she does, making things look as good as they taste. She inherited this skill from her mother, the amazing Sasha Schwerdt, one of the best stylists in the business. We never leave home without a jar of this chutney: it goes with everything and makes a brilliant present as well.

Makes about 1.2kg (enough for 4–5 jars)

thumb-sized piece of fresh root ginger (about 40g), peeled and roughly chopped
4 large garlic cloves, peeled
1 large red onion, peeled and roughly chopped
1 fresh red chilli, chopped, including the seeds
1.2kg tomatoes, cored and chopped

600g granulated sugar
1 tsp dried chilli
1 tsp nigella seeds
1 tsp coriander seeds
1 tsp each salt and freshly ground black pepper
300ml white wine vinegar

Put the ginger, garlic, onion and fresh chilli into a food processor or mini blender and blitz until finely chopped but not completely puréed.

In a large saucepan, ideally a preserving pan, combine the tomatoes, sugar, dried chilli, nigella seeds, coriander seeds and salt and pepper. Add the blitzed garlic mixture, along with the vinegar and stir well.

Bring the mixture to the boil over a high heat. Reduce the heat to low, then cook slowly, still bubbling, until it has thickened and reduced and is sweet, spicy and sticky. This will take 1–1¼ hours. Stir occasionally to make sure it is not sticking to the bottom of the pan.

Sterilise your jars (see page 29). While still warm, pot the chutney into the jars and set aside, uncovered, to cool. When cold, seal tightly, then label and date. Store in the fridge for whenever it takes your fancy.

I offer this chutney as a dipping sauce with Maravic's Spring Rolls (see page 188). It's also great with Gyoza dumplings (see page 118), but in this case stir in 1–2 tablespoons of fish sauce and a good squeeze of lime juice before serving.

Pickled summer cucumbers

We grow our own cucumbers in Devon, and sometimes they work, sometimes they don't. Occasionally, they are so successful that we have a glut, and then pickling is the best way to deal with them. This recipe is from Louisa Carter and works well with veg other than cucumbers: try thinly sliced red or green cabbage, or sliced and blanched green beans. Whatever the veg, the pickle is brilliant for picnics or barbecues as a meat or fish accompaniment.

I have a passion for cucumbers, second only to my love of spinach. There is nothing, I feel, that cannot be enhanced by some cucumber. Pickled cucumbers, which I adore, are an Eastern European speciality. My cousin, Cath Kidston, thinks our family has roots in Eastern Europe, which might explain my predilection.

Makes 3 x
500ml jars

3 large cucumbers, washed and dried
2 medium onions, peeled
2 tbsp salt
600ml white wine vinegar

250g caster sugar
1 tsp fennel seeds
1 tsp coriander seeds

Rest a colander over a large bowl. Thinly slice the cucumbers and onions, sprinkle with the salt and arrange in layers in the colander. Cover with a plate and weigh it down (with a few tins of beans or somesuch) for 3–4 hours. At the end of that time, pour off the excess liquid.

Meanwhile, sterilise your jars and lids (see page 29).

Gently heat the vinegar and sugar in a saucepan until the sugar has dissolved. Add the spices and boil for 10 minutes to create a syrup.

Layer the cucumber and onions into your jars and pour in enough hot syrup to completely cover the contents. Make sure there are no air bubbles, then fasten the lids tightly. Label and date, and leave for at least a week in a cool, dark, airy place. The pickled cucumber will keep for a month or so. Once opened, store in the fridge and use within a week.

'Stone' steak & grilled fish

These are not really recipes, just ideas.

- Stone steak came about originally when one day at the beach we didn't have enough steaks to go around. As usual, I had marinated them in the Steak Marinade on page 202, then Ben barbecued them, but this time he had to make them go further. He therefore put the steaks on a large smooth stone, squeezed over some lemon juice, sliced them at an angle and asked everyone to take some. We all got at least one slice to enjoy with our green salad, asparagus and potato salad. Sharing like this makes complete sense because you can't do more than four large steaks at a time on a bucket barbecue.

- Once the steak and other meats have been cooked, Ben cooks some fish on the embers, which are gentler on the tender flesh. We have a double-sided rack that whole fish (such as mackerel, fresh from the harbour) can be clamped inside for grilling. Sometimes, though, depending on variety or cut, we wrap the fish in foil, with added flavourings, perhaps some marinade (see page 202), and clamp the parcel in the rack for easier turning. This works well with whole sardines or jumbo prawns pushed onto wooden skewers (pre-soaked in water to avoid burning). Fish steaks, such as salmon, tuna, swordfish or monkfish, are good too.

Spiced pickled plums

Another Louisa Carter recipe, this is what you do with the glut of plums that threatens to take over your kitchen. It is infinitely more interesting (and lasting) than stewing them for pudding, although you can use these pickled plums in a crumble. The pickling liquid also works well with fruits such as redcurrants, blackcurrants and cherries. Larger stone fruits, such as apricots, peaches or nectarines, need to be blanched, peeled and halved, then poached in the hot syrup for three minutes before being packed into jars.

These pickled plums would be a perfect accompaniment to something like a pork pie, which you might take on a picnic.

Makes 2
large jars

500g unblemished plums, washed and dried
300ml red wine vinegar
200g soft brown sugar
4 black peppercorns
3 cloves
1 cinnamon stick

First sterilise your jars (see page 29), then keep them warm in a low oven, ready for potting up.

Meanwhile, prick the plums all over with a clean pin.

Heat the vinegar and sugar in a saucepan until the sugar has dissolved, then add the spices and boil for 10 minutes.

Pack the plums into your jars and pour in enough hot syrup to completely cover the fruit. Make sure there are no air bubbles, then fasten the lids tightly. Label and date, then leave in a cool, dark, airy place for at least a week, though a month or two is better. They will keep for a month or so after maturing. Once opened, they will keep for a week if stored in the fridge.

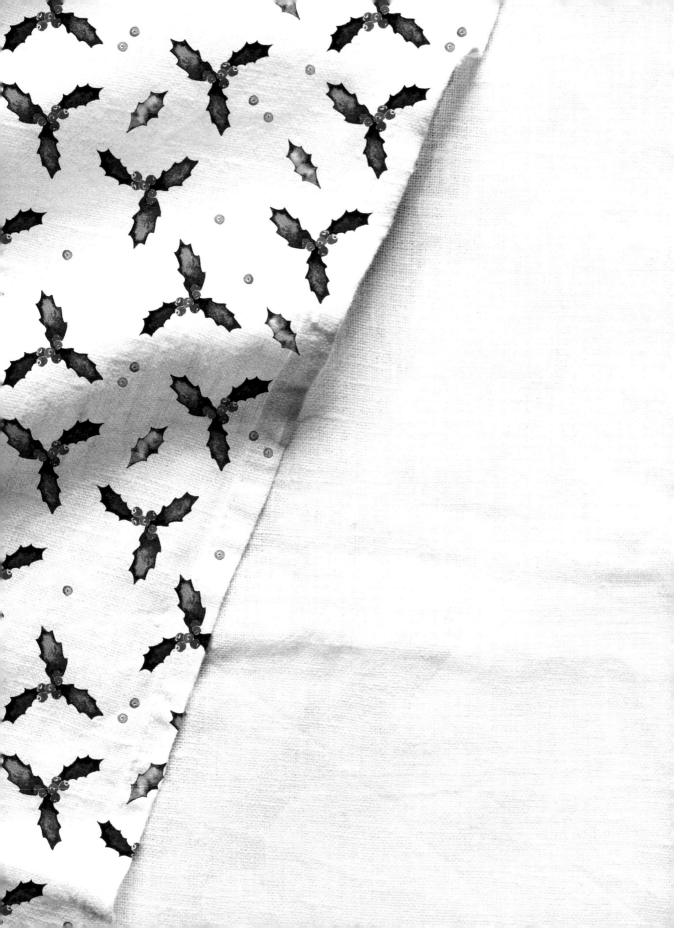

Chapter 8

Christmas

Christmas is one of my favourite times of year, even though it involves lots of work. Like everyone else, I have been guilty in the past of Christmas martyrdom – trying too hard, doing too much, getting super-stressed – but that should be firmly a thing of the past. A few of the following ideas might help as well.

First, be well prepared. Make a list of everyone who is coming and of everything that has to be done in advance (ordering turkey, ham and so on). Plan your menu well, making it as simple as possible – I don't think glamorous food has a place on Christmas Day – and see how much you can actually prepare before the day itself (there are some ideas about that on page 225).

Second, allow yourself plenty of time in which to prepare your Christmas meal. In my family we usually ate around 1.30 so that we were finished before the Queen's speech. In Ben's family, they eat around 5.30, after the Queen. To be honest, I think the latter timing is much better: you can have a leisurely breakfast/ brunch, then have the whole day in which to prepare and cook everything. This allows you some time to actually enjoy your day as well – going to church, opening presents, taking that crisp walk across the park…

And, third, do allow your guests to make a contribution of some sort. You will know what they might be able to offer – perhaps a great sauce (Ben's niece Nancy does her parsley sauce every year to go with the ham), skilful present-wrapping, or arranging table-top flowers – and you should always take advantage of that.

You might want to serve a three-course meal with starter, main course and pudding, but sometimes canapés are a good idea instead of a starter, little mouthfuls of deliciousness that will keep everyone going until the arrival of the turkey. The important thing is to keep them small so they can be eaten in two bites without spilling anything. Many of the recipes throughout this book can be adapted for use as canapés: you could make little fish or chicken goujons, small gyoza dumplings, fish cakes or spring rolls. You could also top toast or crackers with slices of smoked salmon or Gravadlax (see page 214).

Inevitably, Christmas involves leftovers – usually lots of them – but I think of them as a lovely bonus. The key to using leftovers is an understanding that it's not necessary to have a large portion of anything. There's great joy in having a little taste of this and that, so put out those small bowls containing a few bits of cold roast carrot or three curried eggs left over from lunch. My most successful meals are when there are four or five dishes on the table, and everyone's plate is a riot of colour. We call it 'Spanish supper', and treat leftovers like tapas. It is madness for each meal to be brand new, and it can be exhausting.

Whatever you do, enjoy your day. Christmas is a joyous time of year, especially as you will be surrounded by those you love best.

Gravadlax

Salmon is one of my favourite fish, and if it is not grilled on the barbecue by Ben, or baked with loads of garlic and tomatoes (see page 180), I particularly like it smoked, or marinated, as in this recipe. On Christmas morning we often have scrambled eggs topped with smoked salmon, which is actually my second favourite breakfast dish (see page 12). I find smoked salmon very versatile – perfect with cold minted new potatoes in a basic French dressing, and wonderful on toast with a little soured cream. I often do this for Ben as a light supper.

Serves 12, with some leftovers

2 bunches of fresh dill (about 40g in total), roughly chopped
100g sea salt flakes
75g granulated sugar
2 matching sides of salmon, skin on, about 500–600g each
akvavit

2 tbsp white peppercorns or juniper berries, crushed

TO SERVE
small squares of rye bread
soured cream

Place a large sheet of clingfilm on your work surface and sprinkle all over with a third of the dill.

Mix the salt and sugar together, and rub all over both pieces of salmon.

Place one side of salmon, skin-side down, on the dill-sprinkled clingfilm. Cover with another third of the dill, and sprinkle on a few splashes of akvavit, along with the crushed peppercorns.

Place the other side of salmon on top, skin-side up, and cover with the remaining dill.

Bring up the clingfilm and wrap tightly around the two pieces of salmon to make a firm parcel. Put this in a dish or shallow tray and place some heavy weights on top, perhaps a couple of cans. Chill for 48 hours in the fridge, turning the parcel and re-weighting it every 12 hours. Quite a lot of liquid will be released, so make sure the dish is deep enough. Drain the liquid away when turning it over. The finished gravadlax will keep in the fridge for up to 5 days.

To serve, transfer one side of salmon to a board and scrape away as much of the dill marinade as possible. Take a flexible fish knife and carve very thin slices from the thickest end of the fillet. Serve on small squares of rye bread spread first with soured cream.

Roast turkey

Turkey can be dry, undercooked or bland, but if you follow a few easy rules, it will be fine and taste delicious. With all the trimmings, there's no need to cook a huge bird. My first son, Bay, was an enormous 11 pounds 11 ounces at birth. To my way of thinking, any turkey bigger than that is TOO BIG!

Serves 8

1 x 3.5–4kg oven-ready turkey
about 100g butter, softened
4–6 bay leaves
4–6 sage leaves
1 small onion, peeled and quartered
1 lemon, halved
salt and freshly ground black pepper

FOR THE STUFFING
25g butter
1 tbsp olive oil
½ medium onion, peeled and finely
  chopped
300g sausagemeat

30g fresh white or brown breadcrumbs
finely grated zest and juice of ½ lemon
1 tbsp chopped parsley

FOR THE GRAVY (OR SEE PAGE 225)
turkey giblets
1 medium onion, peeled and halved
1 celery stick, chopped
1 carrot, chopped
2 bay leaves
1 tbsp black peppercorns
about 750ml water
25g plain flour
3 tbsp port, sherry or Marsala (optional)

You can start the stuffing the day before. Melt the butter in a medium pan, add the oil and the onion and cook to soften, about 10–15 minutes. Transfer to a bowl, leave to cool, then mix in the remaining stuffing ingredients. Chill overnight.

You can begin the gravy the day before as well by making the stock (but see also the tips for advance preparation on page 225). Roughly chop the giblets and put them in a pan. Add the vegetables, bay leaves, peppercorns and water. Bring to the boil, skim, then cover and simmer for about 1 hour. Strain, discarding all the solids. You will need about 600ml giblet stock for the gravy. Chill overnight.

The next day, take the stuffing and the turkey out of the fridge – you want both to be at about room temperature when the stuffed bird goes in the oven. A good 4½–5 hours before you want to eat, preheat your oven to 220°C/Fan 200°C/Gas 7. Set out a large roasting tin. Cut a large sheet of foil that is long enough and wide enough to line the tin widthways and leave enough overhanging to encase the turkey loosely. Cut another length of foil and arrange this lengthways in the tin, again with enough overhang to fold around the turkey loosely.

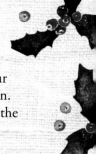

At the neck end of the turkey, loosen the skin over the breast by working your fingers between the skin and flesh as far as you can go. Try not to tear the skin. Divide most of the softened butter between both sides of the breast (to keep the meat succulent). Arrange the leaves attractively between skin and breast.

Put the onion quarters and lemon halves into the cavity of the bird, and season inside and out with salt and pepper.

Spoon the stuffing into the neck end of the turkey, then tuck the skin underneath and keep it in place with little skewers or a couple of cocktail sticks. Tie the turkey with string so that it keeps its shape. Use the remaining butter to smear over the breasts and the legs in particular.

Put the turkey into the roasting tin and loosely fold the sheets of foil over it. Roast for 30 minutes, then lower the temperature to 170°C/Fan 150°C/Gas 3 and continue roasting for about 2½ hours. Baste occasionally, folding the foil back, then replacing it.

Take the turkey out of the oven and remove the foil. Increase the oven temperature to 220°C/Fan 200°C/Gas 7. Pour most of the fat and juices from the tin into a heatproof bowl and set aside. Baste the turkey in what remains in the tin, and roast for another 30 minutes so that the skin browns.

If cooking in the Aga, you could put the turkey tin towards the floor of the roasting oven. Cover the bird with foil and roast for about 1½ hours, basting from time to time. Remove the foil and roast for a final 30 minutes to brown and crisp the skin.

To test if the turkey is cooked, pierce the thigh with a skewer: if the juices run pink, return it to the oven for a few more minutes. If the juices run clear, remove the turkey from the tin, cover with foil and leave to rest for 30 minutes.

Meanwhile, make the gravy. Put 2 tablespoons of the reserved turkey fat into the unwashed roasting tin. Drain the remaining reserved fat into another bowl and keep for frying potatoes; save the dark brown juices for adding to this gravy later. Heat the tin until the fat has melted, then add the flour, stirring until it has picked up all the sticky goodness from the bottom of the pan. Gradually add the alcohol (if using) and the reserved giblet stock, still stirring. When smooth, bring to the boil, then simmer for about 10 minutes. Add the reserved turkey juices to the hot gravy, taste and season with salt and pepper if needed.

Carve the rested turkey and serve with the gravy and all the trimmings – bread sauce, bacon rolls, chipolatas, Creamed Brussels Sprouts (see page 229), carrots, Crushed Roast Potatoes (see page 225) and a spoonful of that delicious stuffing.

Glazed ham

My father's great passion is Anglo-Indian food. He loves curried eggs, a good meat or fish curry, mulligatawny soup, kedgeree, chutneys… I think this all stemmed from his mother, who spent a year in India when she was in her late teens. I have inherited his tastes, liking nothing better than the bite of something flavoured with chilli, ginger and garlic, and I love all curries, whether from the subcontinent or further east. My father also loves ham, and we used to get one each year (alternating with a side of smoked salmon) from his father. Dad prided himself on his carving, and one year he got very perturbed that someone had been sneaking badly cut slices from the ham. It turned out that Dad, who is a terrible insomniac and night eater, had come down in the early hours and carved himself a couple of slices in an uncharacteristically haphazard way, and had not a single memory of it!

These days our ham comes from Phil Spencer, my partner on *Location, Location, Location*. Phil is a man of Kent, his parents and brother farm in Kent, his sister is a vet in Kent, Phil played cricket for the Kent Under-21s, and thus the ham we gratefully receive each year is from Kent! The recipe comes from a Kentish producer too – Farmer Guy (although we have cut the sizes down proportionately here) – and it works every time. We are a large family, but we always have leftovers. These have become traditional now, and we have ham sandwiches, ham and pea risotto, ham in carbonara sauce and croque monsieur (a posh toasted cheese and ham sandwich).

Serves at least 12, with plenty of leftovers

1 x 4.5kg boneless unsmoked gammon joint
equal parts cider, apple juice and water (try 1 litre of each to start with, see method)
1 tbsp cloves, plus extra for garnishing
2 cinnamon sticks

FOR THE GLAZE
60g dark brown sugar
125g honey
1 tsp English mustard powder
2 tbsp wholegrain mustard
sprinkling of cloves
1 cinnamon stick
splash of cider vinegar

Place the ham in a stockpot big enough to hold it comfortably. Pour in enough of the cider mixture to cover it, topping up with more water if necessary, then add the cloves and cinnamon sticks. Bring to the boil, then turn the heat down and simmer with a lid on for about 3 hours 20 minutes to 3 hours 45 minutes, depending on the thickness of the joint.

CONTINUED OVERLEAF ❯

Once the ham is cooked, let it cool a little in the liquid before removing from the pot. Be careful, it will still be hot, so you might prefer to drain off and reserve the liquid first. Set the ham aside until cool enough to handle, then carefully carve off the skin, leaving a thin layer of fat on top of the ham.

Preheat the oven to 180°C/Fan 160°C/Gas 4.

To make the glaze, put all the ingredients, except the vinegar, into a saucepan. Add 1–2 tablespoons of the reserved cooking liquid (enough to get the ingredients wet) and bring to the boil. Continue boiling to reduce a little, then add the vinegar. Keep hot and simmering.

Score the fat on top of the ham in a diamond pattern. Pop the ham into the preheated oven for just 10 minutes to let the fat crisp up a bit.

Take the ham out and spoon over a good helping of the glaze. Pop the ham back in the oven for 10 minutes, until it looks as though the joint is starting to roast – it will be starting to turn golden at the edges. Repeat this process two or three times to suit your taste.

Finally, garnish the ham by studding the centre of each diamond with a clove.

Hot cranberry sauce

This chilli-hot cranberry sauce was invented by Susan McCann for my Christmas book. Susan's west of Scotland business is called SIMPLYaddCHILLI, which is basically what she does – add chilli to everything. She's a girl after my own heart!

A jar of this sauce is a great addition to a hamper you might give as a present, and it will take your Christmas turkey to a whole new level. As a chilli fiend, I add this and any other of Susan's products to omelettes, fish dishes, roast chicken juices, you name it.

If you don't think you're going to eat all of the sauce straight away, freeze half in freezerproof containers, well labelled, and store it for up to three months. Keep the rest in the fridge and use lots of it!

Makes about 1kg

450g cranberries, fresh or frozen
300g red peppers, deseeded and
  roughly chopped
2 whole habañero chillies
3 garlic cloves, peeled

juice of 1 lemon
60ml cider vinegar
100g jam sugar
300g granulated sugar

Put the cranberries, peppers, chillies, garlic and lemon juice into a blender. With the motor running, slowly add the vinegar until the mixture has a thick consistency.

Put both lots of sugar into a large saucepan. Pour in the cranberry mixture and stir well. Bring slowly to the boil, then cook at a rolling boil for about 5 minutes, skimming off any foam that rises to the top.

Pot into sterilised jars (see page 29) and store in the fridge for up to 5 days. Alternatively, freeze as described in the introduction. Enjoy with turkey, chicken or cheese.

Nancy's parsley sauce

Nancy is the daughter of Ben's brother Toby. She works in The Lacquer Chest with her grandmother, and sings with a group called Babeheaven. She will be a star one day. Nancy is also a very good cook. When my father-in-law Viv died, we all went to stay with Gretchen. Nancy had a gig nearby, and everyone went to listen to her (apart from me, as I was babysitting) – a happy occasion in the midst of sadness.

This sauce is delicious with your Christmas glazed ham, but it would also be good with fish or fish cakes, or with a plain cooked vegetable such as broccoli (topped with some grated cheese). You could use chives, chervil, tarragon or dill instead of the parsley.

Serves 6

50g unsalted butter
50g plain flour
500–600ml milk
3–4 heaped tbsp chopped fresh parsley
salt and freshly ground black pepper

Melt the butter in a medium pan. Add the flour and stir in, cooking for about a minute. Remove the pan from the heat and pour in a little milk, stirring well to make a paste. Add a little more milk, then return to a very low heat and gradually add the remaining milk, stirring constantly. You might need to use a whisk if you find any lumps in there.

Increase the heat slightly and bring the sauce to a bubble so that it thickens slightly. Remove from the heat and, if it is too thick, add a little more milk.

Stir in the parsley plus salt and pepper to taste and serve straight away.

Get-ahead tips

Although written with Christmas in mind, these tips could prove useful whenever you are cooking for large numbers.

- VEGETABLES: Blanch your vegetables – broccoli or cauliflower florets, trimmed green beans, slices or chunks of carrot, trimmed Brussels sprouts – in boiling water for just 2–3 minutes. Lift them out with a slotted spoon and plunge straight into a bowl of iced water. This halts the cooking, and helps the vegetables – particularly green ones – to keep their colour. Drain well and place in an ovenproof dish. Brush with a little melted butter or olive oil and cover with foil. Store in the fridge for up to 24 hours.

When it is time to serve the vegetables, preheat the oven to 200°C/Fan 180°C/Gas 6. Season the veg with salt and pepper and brush with a little more melted butter or oil. Cover again with foil and place in the hot oven for 15–20 minutes. The vegetables will be hot, juicy and seasoned, and won't be overcooked.

- ROAST POTATOES: Like the veg above, these too can be prepared and half-cooked up to 24 hours in advance, meaning that they can finish cooking once the turkey is removed from the oven and having its rest.

Preheat the oven to 220°C/Fan 200°C/Gas 7. Peel your potatoes, then boil them in salted water for 5–10 minutes (depending on size). Drain well and return them to the pan. Cover with the lid and shake so that they dry off and become floury. The roughened surface will ensure they become crisp while roasting. Put your chosen fat into a shallow baking tray and place in the oven to heat up. (The best fat to use is hotly debated in our family: Henry swears by goose fat, Sofie by olive oil, I like dripping.) When the fat is smoking hot, add the potatoes, baste well, then roast for 20 minutes. Remove from the oven, turn them over, then drain off as much of the fat as you can (be sure to save it, especially if it's goose fat). Cover the tray of potatoes with foil and leave in a cool place for a maximum of 24 hours. Do not refrigerate.

About 30 minutes before you need the potatoes, or when you take the turkey out of the oven, remove the foil from the tray and finish roasting the potatoes at the same temperature as before for 25 minutes. Drain as usual and serve straight away.

- GRAVY: Here is a fantastic way to cut out the boring job of making gravy on Christmas Day when there are so many other things to do. The principle is that every time you make a poultry roast in the months beforehand, just make a little more gravy than you need and freeze it. Then, when the big day comes, you merely have to defrost the gravy, reheat it, mix in the reduced giblet stock (if you have it) and serve.

Risotto

Like many people of my age, risotto was an early staple, so much so that I went off it for a while. However, in the early 2000s, I went to stay with my uncle and aunt who had rented a house in Positano. There I encountered two dishes that I will always remember: a lemon risotto and a melon ice cream. My inherent desire to fiddle with things and to use leftovers means I am not sure I am ever going to be able to recreate that very plain, pure risotto, but its flavours remain with me still.

Risotto is one of the most comforting of dishes, and is wonderfully therapeutic to cook. You chop your ingredients, then add them gradually, stirring all the time for 20 minutes or so, until the rice is ready. A risotto is the ideal vehicle to use up those inevitable turkey or ham leftovers at Christmas – or anything at any time!

Serves 4–6

1.8 litres stock (homemade or
   from cubes)
3 tbsp olive oil
75g butter
1 large onion, peeled and finely chopped

400g risotto rice
25ml dry white wine
75g Parmesan cheese, freshly grated,
   plus extra for serving
salt and freshly ground black pepper

Put the stock in a large saucepan and heat until boiling. Keep at a simmer while cooking the rice.

Heat the oil and half the butter in another large saucepan, add the onion and cook until softened, about 5 minutes. Pour in the rice, stirring well with a wooden spoon to coat each grain with the oil and butter.

Stir in the wine, which will sizzle and quickly be taken up by the rice. Now start to add the stock a ladleful at a time, stirring until each amount is absorbed by the rice before adding the next. You should end up with rice that is creamy and soft, but still firm to the bite (what the Italians call al dente). This will take about 20–25 minutes.

Just before serving, stir in the remaining butter and the grated Parmesan. Taste for seasoning. Serve with more grated Parmesan to sprinkle on top.

CONTINUED OVERLEAF ❯

Some risotto variations to try...

● LEFTOVER TURKEY RISOTTO

Or leftover anything, really. Add up to 300g leftover turkey to your basic risotto a few minutes before you add your final ladleful of stock (which could be turkey stock, of course). Leftover turkey is also good added to the mushroom risotto below.

● SAFFRON RISOTTO

This is the risotto, flavoured by the most expensive of spices, that is traditionally served with the great Milanese veal dish ossobuco. Simply toast about 10 saffron strands in an old teaspoon over a flame, grind them to a powder and add to the basic risotto while it is cooking. Everything else is the same as above.

● MUSHROOM RISOTTO

Soak 25g dried porcini (ceps) in water for 15 minutes. Drain and chop, saving the soaking water. Meanwhile, clean and slice 350g small mushrooms – chestnut ones are good. Add both types of mushrooms to the onion before the rice, and add the porcini soaking water along with the stock. Proceed as above.

● ASPARAGUS RISOTTO

Clean 500g green asparagus, and break off and discard the hard white stalk at the end. Cut off the tips and set them aside (they should be added at the last moment). Boil the asparagus stalks in water to cover until just tender, adding the tips at the end of the cooking for just a couple of seconds. Drain, keeping the water, which you can add to the stock. Chop the stalks finely and add to the onion when you start cooking the risotto. Serve the risotto decorated with the asparagus tips.

● PEA RISOTTO (OR BROCCOLI, SPINACH, COURGETTE)

Stir 150–200g defrosted frozen peas into the plain risotto, sand cook for a minute or two – perhaps with an extra knob of butter, if needed – until heated through. Stir in loads of freshly grated Parmesan, and perhaps some diced leftover ham.

Creamed Brussels sprouts with marrons glacés

My mother used to cook this, I am sure, but where it came from I know not. She wouldn't have plucked it from thin air. Perhaps it came from my dad, as he is obsessed with marrons glacés and will have them with anything. The combination of Brussels and chestnuts is now fairly traditional as an accompaniment to a Christmas turkey or goose, but the sweetness of the marrons is an interesting take on the original.

You could make the purée the day before, then add the marrons and heat through in a low oven (here the Aga comes into its own) in a dish covered with foil.

Serves 6

500g Brussels sprouts
50g butter
75ml double cream
about 6 marrons glacés, roughly chopped
salt and freshly ground black pepper

As the sprouts will be puréed, you don't need to be all that careful in their preparation. Take off an outer leaf or two, and a slice off the base if it is brown; otherwise leave as they are.

Bring a large pan of water to the boil, add salt and the sprouts, and cook until they are tender, about 8–10 minutes. Drain well, then place in a food processor with half the butter and the cream. Pulse until you have a creamy purée.

Heat the remaining butter in a small frying pan and fry the chestnut pieces until warmed through. Mix these into the sprout purée by hand, then decant into a warmed serving dish. Serve at once.

Boxing Day chutney

What Victoria Cranfield doesn't know about chutneys, jellies and jams quite simply isn't worth knowing. She's won countless medals for her preserves, and kindly gave me this recipe. Chutney is usually made many months in advance to give the ingredients time to combine and mature. This recipe, however, is edible almost straight away, though leaving it for a month does give the best flavour. I gave this chutney to my father once, in a hamper of seasonal goodies. It goes brilliantly with Christmas Day leftovers such as ham, turkey or goose.

Makes 3.6–4kg (about 10–12 jars)

900g onions, peeled and sliced

900g cooking apples, peeled, cored and chopped

300g cranberries

1.2 litres cider vinegar

50g fresh root ginger (unpeeled weight), peeled and finely diced

1 tbsp coarse sea salt

1 tsp mixed spice

finely grated zest of 2 oranges

900g naturally dried apricots, chopped

175g pitted dates, chopped

450g raisins

juice of 8 oranges, or 600ml ready-made orange juice

900g white sugar

Place the first 8 ingredients in a large stainless steel saucepan. Bring gently to the boil, then simmer for about 5 minutes, just until the onions are translucent and the cranberries have popped. You don't want to lose all texture. Remember to stir.

Put the dried fruits into a bowl and pour in the orange juice. Stir well, then set aside for 20 minutes, until the juice has been absorbed.

Add the marinated fruit and the sugar to the onion pan. Bring back to the boil, stirring well, then simmer gently, uncovered, for about 2 hours, giving the mixture a stir now and then. After this time, the liquid rises to the top and the solids sit heavily on the bottom, so it is important to give the chutney a really good stir every 10 minutes or so for the next hour to prevent it catching and burning. After this time it will have cooked down considerably. The chutney is ready when you can draw a spoon through the middle and no excess liquid remains.

Meanwhile, sterilise 10–12 jars and lids (see page 29) and keep them warm.

Spoon or ladle the hot chutney into the jars, filling them as near to the top as possible. Cover with the lids, tightening them only partially. When the chutney is cold, you can tighten them completely. Label and date the jars, and store in a cool, dark place for a month before eating. Unopened jars will keep for up to a year.

My Caribbean Christmas cake

One of the best things about this 'chuck-it-together' cake, which the amazing Rosie Davies taught me how to make and to which I've added my own tweaks, is that you can knock it together the day before you're having guests and decorate it with almonds and a dusting of sugar. (It's lovely during the summer with iced tea and coffee.) If you do want to go the whole hog with marzipan and icing, you can split the work over a couple of days, making the cake the day before you decorate it.

Makes
at least
24 slices

900g of your favourite mixed dried fruit (cranberries, cherries, a vine fruit mix of raisins, sultanas and currants, some extra juicy raisins, apricots and – if you dare – stem or preserved ginger; I used about 300g)

300ml dry cider

225g butter, softened to room temperature

225g soft brown sugar

finely grated zest and juice of 1 lemon and 1 orange

1 tbsp black treacle (optional)

4 large eggs, beaten

225g plain flour

1 tsp ground mixed spice

½ tsp freshly grated nutmeg

170g chopped mixed nuts (almonds, hazelnuts, pecans)

about 6 tbsp apple brandy (or ordinary brandy, whisky, or rum)

FOR THE MARZIPAN

225g ground almonds

180g caster sugar

110g icing sugar, plus extra for dusting

1 large egg, beaten

1 tbsp alcohol (more of the same you used in the cake)

a few drops of vanilla extract, rosewater or orange flower water

FOR THE APRICOT GLAZE

½ jar cheap apricot jam

juice of 1 lemon

FOR THE ROYAL ICING

1kg icing sugar

3–4 egg whites

1–2 tbsp glycerine (available from chemists)

juice of ½ lemon

Preheat the oven to 150°C/Fan 130°C/Gas 2. Line a deep 20cm cake tin or springform tin with baking parchment, which should come well above the rim.

Wash the fruit (if not pre-washed), then chop the larger pieces so they're about the size of the sultanas. Put all the fruit into a large pan with the cider, bring to the boil and simmer for 2–3 minutes. Set aside to cool. The fruit should absorb all the liquid, but if there's any left, drain it off.

CONTINUED OVERLEAF ❯

In a large mixing bowl, cream the butter and sugar with the the orange and lemon zests. Add the treacle (if using). Pour in the beaten eggs and mix well.

Sift the flour with the mixed spice and grated nutmeg and fold into the egg mixture. Now stir in the soaked dried fruit, the chopped nuts and some of the citrus juices to produce a mixture that has a soft dropping consistency. Spoon the mixture into the prepared tin, smooth the top, then make a shallow dent in the middle with a wooden spoon so that the cake will rise evenly as it cooks.

Wrap a thick layer of brown paper or newspaper around the outside of the tin – as high as the lining paper – and secure with string. Place the tin on a baking tray lined with more brown paper and bake for 3–4 hours, checking it halfway through: if the top is getting too brown, cover it with a piece of brown paper.

Check the cake is cooked by inserting a skewer in the middle – it should come out clean. Remove the cake from the oven, prick it all over with a fine skewer and carefully pour the apple brandy into the holes. Allow to cool completely before removing from the tin (about 2 hours). It must be cold before adding the marzipan, or the cake might crumble and the marzipan could melt into a sticky mess.

To make the marzipan, sift the dry ingredients together into a bowl. Add the egg, alcohol and vanilla and mix until you have a pastry-like consistency. Knead until smooth (not too long or it will go oily), then wrap tightly in clingfilm. Set aside to rest in a cool place for at least 1 hour.

Place a large piece of clingfilm on a clean work surface and sift a generous amount of icing sugar over it. Put the chilled marzipan in the middle of the clingfilm and roll it into a circle that is big enough to cover the top and sides of the cake. Use a pastry brush to remove all excess icing sugar.

To make the glaze, put the jam and lemon juice in a saucepan, heat until combined, then push through a sieve to remove the bits. Return the glaze to the pan and continue to simmer until thick.

Turn the cake upside down and brush the flat surface – which will be the top – with the glaze. Place it glaze-side down on the marzipan. Press down lightly to make sure it sticks, then carefully brush the sides of the cake with more glaze, being careful not to slop it over the marzipan. Take a deep breath and lift up both the clingfilm and marzipan all around the cake, smoothing it on to the sides through the film. Make sure it sticks properly.

With the clingfilm still in place, turn the cake right way up and press it firmly all over with your hands. Peel off the film, then trim off any excess marzipan and, if necessary, glue any loose areas with more glaze.

Place the cake on a board and roll a straight-sided jam-jar around the sides to get a really flat vertical surface. If necessary, dust with a little more icing sugar. Allow to dry overnight, or even longer if possible.

To make the icing, sift the icing sugar into a large bowl. Put the egg whites into a separate bowl and whisk until foamy. Gradually add the sifted icing sugar to the whites, whisking slowly at first as the sugar will go everywhere if you mix too fast. Add the glycerine and lemon juice, then beat hard until the mixture is smooth and shiny. It should be the consistency of plaster of Paris.

Press clingfilm directly onto the surface of the icing and set aside for several hours to allow the air bubbles to come out.

When you're ready to apply the icing, place the cake on a turntable, or centre the board on a large saucepan that you can turn to get good coverage. Using a palette knife, spread the icing on the sides of the cake, occasionally dipping the blade into a jug of hot water to make the spreading easier. Ideally, allow the sides to dry overnight before icing the top.

Add any cake-top decorations, such as a sprig of holly, an hour or so after icing, before the surface sets hard. For the perfect finish, tie a bow around your cake.

Christmas pudding

Dense, dark and heavy with booze, Christmas pudding is one of my favourite things. I look forward to eating it every year. Food writer Louisa Carter's recipe can be made and served straight away, which is unusual, or it can be left to mature for a couple of months, which is more traditional. Serve it with Brandy or Rum Butter (see opposite).

Serves 6–8

150g dried sour cherries and/or dried cranberries
300g mixed dried fruit (raisins, sultanas, finely chopped dates)
75ml brandy
juice and finely grated zest of 1 orange
100g softened butter, plus extra for greasing

115g dark muscovado sugar
2 large eggs, lightly beaten
75g self-raising flour
55g fresh white breadcrumbs
50g chopped pecan nuts
1 tsp mixed spice

Place the dried fruit in a saucepan with the brandy, orange zest and juice. Bring to a simmer, then cover and set aside to steep for 30 minutes.

Lightly grease a 1.2–1.4 litre pudding basin with melted butter and place a circle of greaseproof paper in the bottom. Cut 2 sheets of greaseproof paper and 2 sheets of foil each measuring roughly 35 x 35cm. Set aside.

Put the butter and sugar into a large mixing bowl and beat together until pale and fluffy.

Whisk in the eggs one at a time, adding a spoonful of flour between each one if the mixture starts to curdle. Add the soaked fruit and all the juices and stir well to combine. Gently fold in the flour, breadcrumbs, nuts and mixed spice.

Spoon the mixture into the prepared basin and smooth with top with a spatula.

Place the two sheets of greaseproof on top of the two sheets of foil and make a pleat about 4cm wide down the middle – this is to allow for expansion during cooking. Place it over the pudding basin and tie securely with string, making a loop over the top to act as a handle. Trim off any excess paper and foil, or roll it up tightly – it's very important that the greaseproof doesn't come into contact with the water during cooking as it could make the pudding soggy.

Put a trivet, upturned cake tin or dariole mould in a large saucepan and sit the basin on it. Carefully pour in 5–7cm boiling water so it comes just below the bottom of the basin but doesn't actually touch it. Cover the pan with a lid and steam the pudding for 4 hours, topping up the water now and again, as necessary.

If not serving the pudding straight away, set it aside to cool completely, then rewrap it in fresh greaseproof paper and foil and store in a cool, dark place for up to 2 months. To serve, reheat by steaming for 2 hours.

Brandy or rum butter

While brandy is perhaps the more traditional flavouring for a butter sauce to accompany Christmas pudding, I am a great fan of rum. My favourite dark rum at the moment is Duppy Share, and I make cocktails with it, splash it into sauces and use it in my Christmas cake.

One of my earliest Christmas memories is of my grandmother and my father making brandy butter together. My grandfather wasn't drinking at the time, for medical reasons, and my granny, thinking Dad was putting too much brandy in, kept pouring it out. This went on for ages, the two of them standing over the sink and arguing.

Serves 8

125g unsalted butter
150–175g soft brown sugar or icing sugar
about 2 tbsp brandy or rum
freshly grated nutmeg or ground cinnamon (optional)

Cream the butter and sugar together in a bowl using a wooden spoon (or a machine). You want it to be smooth and fluffy.

Slowly blend in the alcohol a few drops at a time. If you like, add a little spiciness with nutmeg or cinnamon. Chill until needed.

Ginger parkin Christmas trees

This recipe has been given to me by James Mackenzie, chef and owner of the Pipe & Glass Inn at South Dalton, East Yorkshire. He has contributed to many of our Christmas shows, and over the years has shared much of his expertise with me. I love the dark, treacly taste of his parkin, and children will love helping you to make these novelty cakes. You'll need a silicone non-stick baking tray containing six or eight tree-shaped moulds. (Each tree should measure 7cm from pointed top to base.) If you want lots, you'll have to make the trees in batches.

Makes 18

150g oats
200g self-raising flour
4 tsp ground ginger
2 tsp freshly grated nutmeg
2 tsp ground mixed spice

200g golden syrup
50g black treacle
200g butter, plus extra for greasing
200g soft brown sugar
2 large eggs, beaten

Preheat the oven to 180°C/Fan 160°C/Gas 4. In a large bowl, mix the oats, flour and spices.

Put the syrup, treacle, measured butter and sugar in a saucepan and melt over a low heat. Whilst the syrup is heating, grease the Christmas tree moulds with the extra butter. Place on a baking sheet.

When the syrup is hot, add the beaten eggs and oat mixture to the pan, and mix well with a wooden spoon. Use this to fill the tree moulds, filling them about three-quarters full.

Bake for 25 minutes, or until the point of a knife comes out clean. The cakes should spring back to the touch.

Transfer the tray to a wire rack and leave to cool for 5 minutes before turning the cakes out of the moulds. Make 2 or 3 more batches of trees in the same way to use up all the mixture.

⟩ TIP ⟨

If your first batch of parkin trees sticks a little in the tray, clean the moulds, then butter and dust with flour for subsequent batches. Don't be too heavy-handed, though – a light dusting is all you need as you don't want the trees to look floury when they come out.

Mince pies

Richard Hunt, nicknamed Peter Kay because he looks just like the comedian, is a giant of a man, and has come back again and again to the Christmas show that we do each year. He is very skilled at what he does, and at passing on that knowledge. He has helped me immeasurably over the years, giving me confidence, which I think is the mark of a true teacher. His scones (see page 143) are wonderful, and so are his mince pies.

Makes 24

60g currants
70g sultanas
70g raisins
70g mixed peel
2 tbsp brandy
1 tbsp Cointreau or orange liqueur
2 tbsp cream sherry
zest and juice of ¼ orange
zest and juice of ¼ lemon
½ tsp mixed spice
50g suet
50g dark soft brown sugar

FOR THE SWEET PASTRY
175g salted butter, at room temperature
85g caster sugar
250g plain flour
1 medium egg

TO SERVE
caster sugar
clotted cream or Brandy Butter
  (see page 237)

To make the mincemeat, put the currants, sultanas, raisins and mixed peel into a medium bowl. Add the brandy, liqueur, sherry, citrus zests and juice and stir everything together. Cover the bowl and leave to soak overnight.

The next day, add the remaining ingredients to the soaked dried fruit and stir well to combine. Pot the mixture into sterilised jars (see page 29) and seal immediately. Store in the fridge or in a cool dark place for up to 6 months. It's best made in advance so that the flavours can meld and mature.

When ready to make your pies, make the pastry. Put the butter and sugar into a food processor and mix together until smooth. Gently add the flour and egg and continue mixing until a soft dough is formed. Do not overwork. Remove the dough from the mixer, wrap in clingfilm and chill for 20 minutes.

CONTINUED OVERLEAF ❯

To assemble the mince pies, have ready two 12-hole non-stick muffin trays. On a lightly floured work surface, gently roll out half the pastry to a thickness of 3mm (the same as a £1 coin). Using a 7.5cm cutter, stamp out circles and use them to line your muffin tin(s). Place in the fridge or freezer for 20 minutes.

Meanwhile, preheat the oven to 200°C/Fan 180°C/Gas 6.

Reroll the remaining dough until 3mm thick (be careful not to overwork it or it will become too soft). Using a 5.5cm star cutter, stamp out lids for your pies. Chill these for 5 minutes or so. If you have only 1 muffin tin, you will have to repeat the rolling and cutting steps once the first batch of pies comes out of the oven.

Remove the lined tin(s) from the fridge and spoon in your mincemeat, about 1½–2 teaspoons per pie. You want them generously filled, but don't overdo it. Place the star lids on the pies and press down gently.

Bake the pies for 15 minutes, until golden brown. You might want to check them halfway through and turn the tray if they're not browning evenly. Leave to cool in the tin for 5 minutes, then use a palette knife to gently remove each pie from its hole and place on a wire rack.

Sprinkle the pies with caster sugar or dust with icing sugar and serve warm with lashings of clotted cream or brandy butter. The pies will keep for up to 5 days in an airtight container, or up to 1 month in the freezer.

Chapter 9

Puddings

While I prefer savoury to sweet, I do appreciate puddings, particularly those involving fruit or dark chocolate. Actually, now I think about it, if you put apple crumble and custard in front of me, I wouldn't say no.

I have recently come to the conclusion that we have got fruit and vegetables the wrong way round. We tend to cook vegetables and eat fruit raw, but many vegetables actually taste better raw, and a number of fruits are much more delicious when cooked. So when I am considering what pudding to serve, I will more often than not plump for fruit. It's simplicity itself to offer huge bowlfuls of fresh raspberries or strawberries, but often, particularly with stone fruit, I will bake or fry it, either plainly, or with something on top or in its cavity, and serve it with ice cream perhaps. I also sometimes make a straightforward fruit salad such as I might serve at breakfast (see page 30), but add some alcohol to enhance the flavours (my current favourite is satsumas and gin). Whatever the pudding, though, I will always offer it with bowls of whipped double cream (or clotted cream when in Devon) and plain yoghurt.

By pudding time, people are well fed, feeling sociable, and there will be lots of conversation and laughter. I like to keep people sitting at the table, and having a pudding keeps the good time going. In the summer I usually serve a light main course with a more substantial pudding. These two courses are punctuated by salad and cheese, the French way of doing things, which allows me to go and prepare the pudding while people are still nibbling. Sometimes, though, to avoid disappearing, I like to make a pud that can be taken straight from fridge to table so I can chat for longer. (In winter, I change the courses, serving a soup first, then mains, then pud.)

Most puddings can be made in advance, which means you have more time to spend with your guests. I am never without airtight plastic boxes of meringues – everyone loves them and they are not difficult to make (see page 250). If in perfect shape, they can quickly be filled with a flavoured cream and berries. If they are a bit broken, I mix them up with whipped cream for an Eton mess. A cake, jelly or mousse can also be made the day before. There are only a few recipes that require last-minute attention, but I don't resent the time spent chopping, turning or whipping: I love being in my kitchen, and it's especially satisfying if I can hear a happy buzz of conversation from the dining table.

I have only a few pudding recipes that I serve on a regular basis, and I would quite often be happy to serve as a pudding-cum-cheese course what many would think of as a starter. A good pear, for example, is wonderful thinly sliced and served with rocket and Manchego. I once bought a box of fresh figs and served them, broken up, with chunks of mozzarella, sprinkled with sea salt flakes and extra virgin oil. If I'd had some prosciutto, that would have been added too. A great starter, you might say, but for me it could easily be an even greater pudding.

Lemon & polenta cake

Here's a wonderful cake that could be served for pudding or for afternoon tea. The recipe was kindly given to me by Carla Simao of Tea's Me, my regular breakfast haunt.

Polenta (cornmeal) is an interesting ingredient when used in baking. It adds texture and flavour, as do the ground almonds, with their melting sweetness. Since the cake is completely flourless, it's great for coeliacs and others who can't tolerate gluten. (You can buy gluten-free baking powder as well.)

Serves 12

200g unsalted butter, plus extra
    for greasing
175g caster sugar
200g ground almonds
150g fine polenta
1 tsp vanilla extract

3 large eggs
juice and finely grated zest
    of 2 small lemons
1 tsp baking powder
pinch of sea salt
icing sugar, for dusting

Preheat the oven to 190°C/Fan 170°C/Gas 5. Butter a 20cm round springform cake tin, and line it with baking parchment. Place on a baking sheet.

Put the butter and the sugar into a bowl and beat together with an electric whisk for 10 minutes. Gradually add the almonds and polenta, along with the vanilla, and whisk for another 2 minutes.

Add the eggs to the mixture and beat until fully combined.

Finally, add the lemon juice and zest, the baking powder and salt. Mix well.

Pour the mixture into the prepared cake tin and bake for 50 minutes, or until dark golden on top and a skewer inserted into the centre comes out clean.

Place the tin on a wire rack and leave the cake to cool completely before releasing it and removing the parchment.

Dust with icing sugar and serve warm or cold with berries and whipped cream, crème fraîche or Greek yoghurt.

Individual meringues

When I have spare egg whites (after making mayo or hollandaise, for instance), I like making meringues (if I haven't already used them to make a whisky sour, Ben's favourite cocktail). I store them in plastic boxes ready for the weekend (or freeze them, separated by paper, for up to three months). I think the recipe I used originally was from a Nigella book, but all meringue recipes are very similar – there are only two major ingredients after all.

You can vary the meringues in many ways. The ones here are pure white in colour, but you could use golden caster sugar for a yellower result. If you fancy marbled meringues like those you see in Ottolenghi's or Carluccio's windows, dip a metal skewer into your chosen food colouring, then swirl it through the basic mix – you want only the merest streaks of colour. I use a tablespoon to make individual meringues, but you could pipe them using an icing bag with a star nozzle for a different look. For a softer internal texture, more like a pavlova, add a teaspoon each of cornflour and white wine vinegar as you are whipping the whites.

Makes 12–14

3 large egg whites (the eggs should be very fresh, as this makes separating yolks and whites much easier)
pinch of salt
225g caster sugar

FOR THE CREAM

400–500ml double cream
1–2 tsp vanilla extract
1–2 tsp maple syrup

Preheat the oven to 150°C/Fan 130°C/Gas 2. Line 2 baking sheets with baking parchment.

Make sure your mixing bowl and whisks are spotlessly clean. Any speck of grease (even a spot of egg yolk in the whites) would make it very difficult to whisk them to the volume you need. As a precaution, you could wipe the bowl and beaters with a slice of lemon if you like.

Put the egg whites and salt in the bowl and whisk on a low speed for a couple of minutes. Turn the speed up to medium and whisk for another few minutes. Once the whites are fluffing up well, turn the speed to high and whisk until they form stiff peaks. This means they should cling to the sides of the bowl and not fall out if the bowl is turned upside down over your head. Take care that they're not dry and

CONTINUED OVERLEAF ❯

overwhisked, though, or it will be difficult to whisk in the sugar and the volume will collapse.

Now start adding the sugar a tablespoonful at a time. (Many recipes sing the praises of heating the sugar before adding it, but I never bother.) Keep beating at high speed while the sugar is being added. This should take about 5–10 minutes, after which the meringue mix will be stiff and wonderfully glossy.

Place tablespoons of the meringue mixture on the prepared baking sheets, spacing them well apart.

Put the sheets in the oven and immediately lower the temperature to 140°/Fan 120°/Gas 1. Close the door and bake for 45–60 minutes. Turn off the oven, prop the door slightly ajar (you can use the handle of a wooden spoon), and leave the meringues until they and the oven are cold.

When you're ready to serve, whip the cream with the flavourings. Sandwich the meringues together if you like, but I usually put a meringue on a plate with a spoonful of cream and some berries, or some cooked fruit (see page 262) or something like an apple purée.

Blood orange jelly

This is a blast from childhood, but I was recently reminded of the joys of jelly when my friend Magnus served me one for dinner. It's so easy, and delicious.

That experience encouraged me to dig out my great-great granny's recipe for jelly, which sounds so funny now: 'Colour and flavour some common jelly with crème de menthe. When strawberries are in season, lay a foundation of big strawberries on a layer of strawberry ice. Cover with the jelly.'

In the old days, jelly would have been made in moulds, which I really love, but Ben says they don't work, so I don't buy them any more. However, I do have an old plastic mould that used to belong to my mum. It is in the shape of a bunny rabbit – surely every household had one? – and jelly made in that is strictly for the family. For posher gatherings I make jelly in my vintage stemmed crystal bowls, which are perfect for lunch or dinner parties and fantastically kitsch.

The recipe below is completely straightforward, but you can add fruit if you like. Pour a little of the dissolved jelly into the dishes, let it set, then top with some chopped fruit and a little more dissolved jelly. Back in the fridge, and repeat this process until all the jelly and fruit are used up, and the dishes are full. Serve with ice cream or condensed milk. (The first time I gave my stepsons condensed milk, they told their mum they really liked the new kind of milk they'd had at Dad's house, and she rang me to say she'd been trying for years to get them on to goat's milk. I did eventually confess the truth.)

Serves 8

2 x 135g packets of orange jelly
450ml boiling water
600ml blood orange juice

Break the jelly into cubes and place in a large heatproof bowl. Pour in the boiling water and stir until the jelly has completely dissolved. (I use less water than suggested on the packet in order to make the blood orange flavour even stronger.) When the jelly is cold but not set, pour in the blood orange juice, give it a stir, then pour the mixture into your chosen mould(s). Put in the fridge or a cool place to set.

When ready, you could decorate each serving with a swirl of whipped cream, a spoonful of condensed milk and a pretty sweet biscuit stuck on top. If serving from a large mould, a scoop of ice cream would go well beside a spoonful or two of jelly.

Blackberry & apple crumble

Where I was brought up, in the country, there were endless hedgerows, and we always picked blackberries from them. About fourteen years ago, I really overdid it when making *Location, Location, Location*, and I got what they call 'walking pneumonia'. I took ten days off work and went to my parents' house in Dorset. There was just me and my border terrier Foxy, so I began my recovery by watching the first three series of *West Wing* back to back. I also went on long walks and picked blackberries – loads of them – and made lots of lovely things, including blackberry vodka, blackberry jam and jelly, and blackberry and apple crumble. These days, however, a family berry-picking expedition with the four boys means we rarely make it home with a single blackberry, so we end up eating apple crumble.

Serves 6

700g Cox's apples, cored and
    cut into wedges
300g blackberries
juice of 1 orange
1 tsp ground mixed spice
3 tbsp light soft brown sugar

FOR THE TOPPING
175g plain flour
100g butter, chopped
50g light soft brown sugar, plus an
    extra tablespoon for sprinkling
50g regular rolled oats

Preheat the oven to 200°C/Fan 180°C/Gas 6.

Put the apples into a bowl with the blackberries, orange juice, mixed spice and 2 tablespoons of the sugar. Mix well, then spoon into a shallow ovenproof dish.

To make the topping, put the flour into a large bowl and rub in the butter. Stir in the sugar and oats, then spoon the mixture over the fruit in a thin layer. Sprinkle the remaining tablespoon of sugar over the crumble.

Bake for 40 minutes, until the crumble is golden brown and the fruit underneath it has softened. Serve with custard.

Fruit fool

Once upon a time, fruit fools consisted of puréed stewed fruit folded into a sweet custard. Thank goodness cream is now used instead of the custard (I haven't quite mastered the recipe for that, but Waitrose has). The first fools I tasted were made by Amabel Lindsay, a friend of my parents. She cooked for the masses, having loads of teenagers, and would serve fool inside a frozen bowl made of ice and flowers. I thought it was the prettiest thing I had ever seen. I serve my fools in some of my antique bowl collection, and I am very partial to a fool that is pink (probably because I am always surrounded by men).

The fruit used is up to you. Sour types, such as rhubarb, gooseberries and blackberries, have to be cooked beforehand. Sweet ones, on the other hand – strawberries, raspberries and suchlike – can be used raw, and even when they are past their best. Simply chop or crush them (you could sieve the raspberries to make a coulis-like sauce) and fold through the cream/yoghurt mixture so that the fool looks marbled. Save some perfect fruit to decorate the top.

Serves 6

500g rhubarb, gooseberries or blackberries
50–100g caster or icing sugar (quantity
    depends on the sweetness of the fruit)

squeeze of lemon or orange juice
450ml double cream
100g Greek yoghurt

Prepare the fruit as necessary: trim and wash the rhubarb stalks and cut into rough chunks; top and tail the gooseberries and give them a good wash; hull the blackberries and wash very briefly.

Place the chosen fruit in a large stainless steel pan and add the sugar to taste. Squeeze in a little citrus juice, then cover and bring to a simmer. Turn the heat down low and continue simmering until the fruit is tender and cooked. Taste and add a little more sugar if necessary. Set aside to get cold.

Blitz the cold fruit in a blender, and then, if you can be bothered, push through a sieve. (I would do this with the gooseberries and blackberries, not the rhubarb, but the choice is yours.)

Put the cream and yoghurt in a bowl and whisk until thick. Using a metal spoon, fold in the cold fruit. Divide among 6 small glasses, then chill for about an hour. Serve with a nice biscuit.

Crème brûlée

One of my oldest friends is Turkish, and very handsome indeed. Many years ago we were having dinner in a restaurant in Istanbul. My friend went to the loo and the waiter took my order for dessert. I left the table too, and when I came back, my crème brûlée had arrived, and there was a little handwritten note attached: 'You need this like a hole in the head.'

Perhaps surprisingly, I'm still very fond of my friend, and my love for crème brûlée is undimmed. Ben and I both make it occasionally, but we and the boys all order it whenever we eat out.

Serves 6

500ml double cream
2 tsp vanilla extract
6 large egg yolks
40g golden caster sugar, plus extra for sprinkling

Pour the cream into a heavy-based pan and add the vanilla extract. Place over a medium heat just until bubbles start to appear around the edge. Take off the heat and set aside.

Using a spoon, stir the egg yolks and caster sugar together in a large bowl until they form a cream. (Using a whisk would incorporate too much air and make the mixture mousse-like.)

Preheat the oven to 150°C/Fan 130°C /Gas 2. Stir the warm cream into the egg yolk mixture to combine, then transfer to a bowl and place over a pan of simmering water, making sure the bowl doesn't actually touch the water. Allow to cook very gently until the mixture has thickened slightly and coats the back of a spoon.

Divide the mixture equally between six 150ml ramekins. Place in an ovenproof tray and pour enough hot water around them to come just under halfway up the sides. Bake for 20 minutes. Remove from the tray, allow to cool, then chill overnight.

The next day, sprinkle each dish with a little caster sugar, tilting it around to distribute evenly. Preheat the grill until very hot, then put the dishes under it until the sugar has caramelised. This step can be done with a blowtorch, if you have one, but take care not to focus on one spot or it may burn. Allow to cool, then serve.

Chocolate & coffee mousse

My first-ever dinner party, when I was a teenager, took place at home. The menu was prawn salad in avocado for a starter, roast chicken with peas, stuffed baked potato and bread sauce from a packet, with chocolate mousse for pudding. My mum did it all, and we also had three bottles of Piat d'Or between the six of us. However, Mum suddenly had to go to London, and we were left in the hands of the Australian au pair. Before leaving, Mum told me firmly that in her absence, the boys should be told they could no longer stay the night. In all the excitement, I forgot to ring two of the boys, and they duly arrived, complete with sleeping bags. I thought it would be OK and squared it with the au pair. So we dined magnificently, drank our wine, and then played sardines – all really innocent and fun!

The next morning the boys were picked up by their mothers before mine came home. But within minutes of her arrival, one mother phoned to thank Mum for having her son to stay. Mum's face as she said, 'It was a pleasure,' was a picture.

Serves 6

125g dark chocolate (70% cocoa solids)
25ml espresso coffee
1 tbsp rum

3 medium eggs, separated
1 tbsp maple syrup
2 squares good-quality white chocolate

Break up the pieces of dark chocolate and put them into a heatproof bowl. Add the espresso and rum, then sit the bowl over a pan of simmering water, making sure it doesn't actually touch the water. Stir occasionally.

As soon as the chocolate has melted, take the pan off the heat and take the bowl off the pan. Allow to cool for 2–3 minutes, then stir in the egg yolks and maple syrup.

Whisk the egg whites in a spotlessly clean bowl until they stand in soft peaks, i.e. set enough not to slip around the bowl and to remain in it if you hold it upside down over your head.

Using a metal spoon, fold one spoonful of egg white into the chocolate mixture, then carefully fold in the remainder until the mixture is smooth. Divide between 6 espresso cups or small glasses. Chill for 2 hours.

Take the mousses out of the fridge. Finely slice the white chocolate into shavings, sprinkle a few over the top of each mousse and serve.

Pan-fried fruit

I often refer to this recipe as my tarte tatin, only it doesn't have any pastry and it isn't baked! Basically, I pan-fry the fruit with minimal additions, shape it into a circle and serve it with bowls of cream or yoghurt. Although I generally make it with one type of fruit, a mixture of peaches, nectarines and plums is really good.

Serves 4

8 plums, greengages or apricots,
   or 4 peaches or nectarines
2 tbsp unsalted butter
2 tbsp caster sugar

FOR THE SALTED CARAMEL SAUCE
75g white granulated sugar
3 tbsp water
300ml double cream
100g soft light brown sugar
good pinch of salt

First make the salted caramel sauce. (The recipe makes 350g, but only a little is needed here, so save the rest in the fridge for topping ice cream, fruit, rice pudding, brownies or cake, and use within 5 days.) Put the white sugar and water into a large, heavy-based pan and place over a low heat until the sugar dissolves. Increase the heat slightly and cook, without stirring, until the sugar starts to caramelise. It will begin by turning golden at the edges, then the colour gradually works its way to the middle. Give the pan a shake if it looks like one side is becoming too dark; if it burns, the sauce will taste bitter. Once the sugar has caramelised satisfactorily, pour in the cream, standing at arm's length, as it will splutter. Stir well – the caramel might set hard, so if it does, just continue to cook over a low heat until it melts back into a sauce. Stir in the brown sugar, then whisk well. Bring to a simmer and cook for 2–3 minutes. Stir in the salt, taste it and add more if you wish. Keep warm while you prepare the fruit.

Cut all the fruits in half and discard the stones. Slice the larger fruit into pieces the same size as the plum halves. I think quarters are easier to handle in the pan.

Melt the butter in your frying pan until quite hot, add the fruit and sprinkle with the caster sugar. Cook for a few minutes until the underside is nicely brown, then flip over and brown the other side. You want the fruit pieces to look pretty.

Swirl the fruit around in the buttery mixture, then arrange neatly in a flattish bowl (making concentric circles will make it look like a tarte tatin). Drizzle 1 or 2 tablespoons of the very rich salted caramel sauce over the top. Serve with whipped double cream, flavoured if you wish, or Greek yoghurt.

Chapter 10

Cocktails
& Drinks

People often ask me whether there is anything I have made for television that I continue to enjoy in my day-to-day life. Well, I still cook a lot of the recipes I was taught by numerous experts, but my favourite lessons have been learning to make cocktails. Of course, I am very aware that alcohol is a contributory factor in breast cancer, so I regularly go days or even weeks without a drink. However, I adore mixing a good cocktail for my friends.

Since my interest began, I have become quite a dab hand at mixing, shaking and pouring. I've acquired the whole kit and caboodle necessary for the art: the basics are a shaker, strainer, lemon press and jigger measure, but useful extras, such as muddlers and special mixing spoons, can be found online. Just as vital, though, is ice, so make sure you have a selection of ice-cube trays.

I also own several cocktail books, and these made me aware of the cardinal rule of cocktail-making: there has to be a balance between the various components of a cocktail – the strong and the weak, the sour and the sweet. Spirits, such as gin or vodka, are strong; liqueurs, such as Cointreau and crème de menthe, are (relatively) weak; sour is obviously lemon or another citrus fruit; and sweet is sugar, syrup or honey.

But there are many drinks I make apart from cocktails. If I am having a Bonfire Night party, I serve mulled cider, which is perfect for a crowd on a cold night. I love limoncello, the Italian vodka-based liqueur, and homemade is by far the best (see page 276). It can be drunk after dinner, but could also be poured over ice cream, a fruit salad, berries or cake.

I'm also a big fan of my great-great granny's damson gin: 'Fill large wide-necked bottles two-thirds full with damsons that have been pricked all over with a silver fork. The remaining third of the bottles to be filled with lumps of sugar. Add as much gin as the bottles will hold, cork well and leave for three months, after which time strain off the liquid and put in wine bottles.' The method might be old-fashioned, but it works wonderfully well.

Of course, there are many delicious drinks that don't contain alcohol. I try to make elderflower cordial every year when the trees bear their umbrella-like flowers. Diluted with water, it makes a wonderfully refreshing drink (see page 280). I also like iced teas in the summer, and am very keen on flavoured waters. Fill a jug with water and let it sit for a while to allow any chlorine to dissipate; then add a flavouring, such as slices of citrus fruit, or sprigs of rosemary, or even coils of cucumber peel. Put in the fridge until cold. Much nicer than drinking plain tap water.

I also recommend you try my great-great-granny's recipe for lemon water: 'Peel off the rind of a fresh lemon as thin as possible. Add one lump of sugar and pour on it a quart and a half of boiling water. Strain when cold and chill on the ice.'

Aperol spritz

I first had this refreshing Italian drink around the time I learnt to make a quick carbonara (see page 116). You can always recognise the bright orange colour of Aperol, a slightly bitter low-alcohol liqueur (11%) made from a mixture of herbs and fruit flavours, including rhubarb. It is generally mixed with soda water to make a spritzer, which means you can drink quite a lot without getting too squiffy. I made huge jugs of the more alcoholic version below for my sister's hen party, which went down very well.

Serves 1

a few ice cubes
1–2 parts Aperol (this is bitter, so less is best)
3 parts Prosecco
splash of soda water
1 orange slice

Put the ice cubes into a large wine glass and add the liquids one by one. There will be a layer of orange Aperol at the bottom of the glass, then the clearer look of prosecco and ice. Stir together, then top with the orange slice.

Vodka martini

The classic martini is made with gin, but I love it with vodka, as does James Bond. Like him, I also prefer it shaken rather than stirred.

The vodka that I use now is Black Cow, the invention of Ben's friend Paul Archard, who moved to Dorset and couldn't get over the waste involved in milk production. On investigating what could be done, he began making cheese from the curds of unwanted milk, and vodka from the whey. The finished vodka is brilliantly packaged in what looks like an old glass milk bottle, and it has a gold top.

Serves 1

½ part dry vermouth
2 parts Black Cow vodka
ice cubes
1 green olive or a strip of lemon zest

Chill your martini glass, either in the fridge or freezer, or simply fill it with ice for a minute or two.

Quite often, I have to admit, I add the vermouth to the chilled glass, swirl it around and then pour it out. The martini is then very pure. However, it's more conventional to combine the vermouth and vodka in a cocktail shaker, fill it with ice and stir or shake for a few seconds until the liquid is chilled.

Strain into a chilled martini glass. Garnish with the olive speared on a cocktail stick, or add a twist of lemon peel.

Negroni

I first encountered this feisty cocktail at a party, when I was encouraged to try it for Dutch courage in order to face an ex-boyfriend who was there too. Three glasses in, I had the requisite confidence.

When asked by my father a few Christmases ago what I would like for a present, I said, 'Negroni ingredients and recipes.' He duly presented me with a very nice bottle of vermouth and a copy of *The Negroni* by Gary Regan. When the bottle was finished, I went back to Hedonism Wine for more. I found out it was very expensive, so I had been serving my friends rather pricey cocktails! With regret, I bought a slightly cheaper version.

Serves 1

ice cubes
1 part gin
1 part Campari
1 part sweet vermouth (usually red)
wedge of orange or a sliver of orange peel

Put a few ice cubes into a tumbler or whisky glass and add the liquids. Stir together, then garnish with orange wedge or peel.

Will's apple margarita

Ben's greatest friend Will was giving a party to celebrate his fiftieth birthday, so I invented this cocktail in his honour – a combination of tequila, elderflower liqueur, apple and lime juice – and undertook to provide enough for the party. After filming of the Christmas show down in Devon had finished, I lined up my wonderful assistant Beth and the rest of the team in the kitchen, giving them each a different job – measuring, pouring, mixing, decanting into empty apple juice bottles (I used my own apple juice). We had a good production line going.

Like all cocktails, however, its success depends on the ice and the chilling. Nobody had told the party organisers about this, so when we arrived at the event in London some time after the bulk delivery of unchilled margarita, we found people drinking the cocktail warm in wine glasses. We swiftly moved into action in pursuit of ice to render the cocktail more drinkable.

Serves 1

2 parts good-quality tequila
¾ part St Germain Elderflower Liqueur
1½ parts apple juice
squeeze of fresh lime juice
pinch of finely crushed sea salt
ice cubes

TO SERVE
salt
slice of lime

Pour all the liquids into a cocktail shaker. Fill it with ice, and stir or shake for a few seconds until the liquid is chilled.

Strain into a chilled, salt-rimmed glass with a slice of lime to garnish.

Limoncello

For the Christmas show, we made quite a few bottles of limoncello – a couple to be broached and tasted, most of them to be saved for possible photography later on. This time, though, there was not a bottle left. I have never seen anything disappear so quickly!

A bottle of homemade limoncello makes a fantastic present at any time of year. It feels so celebratory, and reminds me of hot days in the Italian sunshine, and several evenings in Venice.

Makes about
2 litres

juice and finely grated zest of 8 unwaxed lemons
800g granulated sugar
650ml water
1 litre vodka

Place the lemon zest in a large pan with the sugar and water. Heat gently until the sugar dissolves, then increase the heat slightly and simmer for 15 minutes. Set aside until lukewarm.

Add the lemon juice and vodka to the pan, then cover and leave the liquid to infuse for a week.

Using a sieve lined with muslin or kitchen paper, strain the liquid into a large jug. Decant into sterilised bottles (see page 29), seal tightly and add a pretty label with the date. It should keep for about six months, but you'll probably run out of it long before that.

Mulled cider

Andy Thompstone of Thompstone's Devonshire Cider showed me how to make this mulled cider for my Christmas show a couple of years ago. Usually for these shows, we have to try and make it all look very cold and Christmassy, even in places like Switzerland and Finland. But that particular day, in England, it was the most authentic cold we had ever experienced, and the warm cider disappeared at a rate of knots!

It's a fair bet that everyone is familiar with mulled wine, but this cider is just as celebratory. I make it for Bonfire Night, but it's good from September through until Christmas – and after.

Makes 8 litres

8 litres good-quality dry cider

60g ground cassia or 3 cinnamon sticks, crushed

2 tbsp allspice berries, crushed

2 tsp ground star anise

2 tsp ground cloves

2 tbsp peeled and grated fresh root ginger

2 pinches freshly grated nutmeg

275g dark muscovado sugar (less if using sweet cider)

180–250ml rum, to taste

apple slices, cinnamon sticks and whole star anise, to garnish

Pour the cider into a large, heavy-based pan and warm over a medium heat.

Add all the spices and sugar, then carefully bring the mixture up to 60°C. If you go over that, you run the risk of boiling off the alcohol.

Take the pan off the heat, cover with a lid and allow to steep for at least a few hours. The longer you leave it, the spicier the drink.

Add as much rum as you dare, then strain the liquid to get rid of the spices. Your cider is now ready to drink. Add your garnishes, then simply reheat – again very gently – and enjoy.

Elderflower cordial

This elderflower cordial, taught to me by Rosie Davies, is one of the nicest things I have ever made, and also really easy, so long as you can get hold of the elderflower heads in spring. This recipe includes tartaric acid, which is a natural preservative (originally found on the inside of wine barrels), so it improves the keeping quality of the cordial. Epsom salts are included to balance the acidity of the citric and tartaric acids, and it is the balance that makes this cordial so more-ish. (Both the acids can usually be obtained from a local chemist; if not, Lakeland or Wilkinson's should have them, or you can get them online.)

We made quite a few bottles of this lovely cordial for one of my shows, but Bay got addicted and the cordial was disappearing far too fast for my liking. When there was only one bottle left, I squirrelled it away from him so I could enter it for the Chagford Show.

Makes about 1.5 litres

6–8 young elderflower heads
3–4 large unwaxed lemons
1kg granulated sugar
25g citric acid

15g tartaric acid
15g Epsom salts
900ml boiling water
lemon slices or mint sprigs, to serve

Gently rinse the elderflowers in cold water. Drain well.

Wash and dry the lemons, then grate the zest finely into a very large and thoroughly clean bowl. Squeeze in the lemon juice, then add the sugar, acids, Epsom salts and elderflowers. Pour in the boiling water and stir until the sugar has completely dissolved. Cover and leave until cold, preferably overnight.

Strain through a very fine sieve or muslin. Using a funnel, pour into sterilised bottles (see page 29). Seal tightly, label and date, then store in a cool place.

To serve, dilute the cordial to taste with sparkling water and serve over ice with a slice or two of lemon or a sprig of mint floating on top. For grown-ups you could add a shot of gin or vodka, or mix it with white wine and sparkling water to make an elderflower spritzer. Once the bottle is open, store in the fridge. It will keep for about 6 months.

Grange iced tea

Iced teas are delicious, and you can have them with or without alcohol. We drink them a lot during balmy summers and autumns. At Grange we make iced tea with home-pressed apple juice, which is especially enticing. Do be careful, though, if re-using empty apple juice bottles for storing your alcoholic iced tea: a couple of times we have given the children some by mistake. The moral? Always label clearly.

Basically, you want equal parts of cold tea and apple juice, with a proportion of lemon juice according to taste. You can sweeten it if you like, but you must add loads of ice, lemon slices and mint. I like to use Barry's Irish breakfast tea, which is mostly Assam with a strong, malty flavour (get it at Sally Clarke's or online), but Yorkshire tea is good as well.

Make your iced tea in a large jug, and if your guests would like it with some alcohol – probably vodka or gin – you can add it separately. Enjoy!

Makes 2.2 litres (serves about 12)

1 litre water
2 teabags (breakfast, builder's, probably not Earl Grey)
1 litre clear or cloudy apple juice (ours is always cloudy)

4 lemons, 2 juiced, 2 sliced
clear honey, to taste (optional)
lots of ice
lots of mint sprigs

Boil the water. Put the teabags in a large heatproof jug and pour the water over them. (I once wrecked an ordinary glass jug by combining hot tea with ice, so use a heatproof bowl if you don't have a suitable jug.) Leave to steep for 5 minutes, then remove the bags. Set aside to get cold.

When the tea is cold, mix with the apple juice and lemon juice. If it is too tart for you (I love a good pucker), add a little honey. Mix in the ice, the sliced lemons and mint. Serve, offering alcohol on the side if your guests would like it.

Index

Acknowledgements

There are hosts of people without whom this book just would not exist and to whom I am immensely grateful. First all the chefs who have inspired me and kindly allowed me to include their recipes in this book, including all those who have stuck with me over the years and taught me so much in the making of the TV craft shows.

Then there is everyone at Hodder, Nicky Ross and Sarah Christie. It was their belief that I had this book in me that drove this project forward. The amazing team who worked so hard to make this book look as it does, Nikki Dupin and Rita Platts, who agreed to be dragged down to Devon and remained true to my belief that this book would only work if it featured our home. Seeing all my old favourites so beautifully photographed has been an enormous pleasure; this is my real kitchen. That said it is incredibly important that my way of doing things can be translated onto your plate, and for that I need to thank Emma Marsden, who ensured everything made sense, as a bit of this and a bit of that doesn't quite make the grade. Thanks also to Trish Burgess, who edited faithfully and was so patient with my constant tweaks.

To my mother-in-law Gretchen Andersen, who is a hugely inspirational figure in my life and whose shop and hiring outlet, The Lacquer Chest, is a Mecca for all food stylists. Long may it thrive. To everyone at Raise the Roof, who continue to find wonderful people to share their talents on TV, and to IWC who began the beginning. To Heather, Chrissie, Maravic, Angelina and Angie, whose team effort keeps life running smoothly: I do not do it all. To my sister Natasha, who when told about this book said, 'Will it be called "Go to Ottolenghi, Buy Food, Come Home, Eat It"?' To my sister Sofie, who is a better cook than me, and to my brother Henry, who thinks he is. To my dad, from whom I inherited my taste buds and my love for chilli, mustard, chutney, crustaceans and pork pie. To Hilary and Annie at Arlington Enterprises, and Luigi who, quite rightly, stops me doing stuff for free. To Lisa McCann, who is proof positive that the best things come in small packages; we have come a long, long way together. But, as it turns out that cookbooks don't just happen, and especially not to people like me, who will find a thousand reasons not to sit down and get on with it, I am most grateful to Beth Wilmont and Sue Fleming. Beth's patience, attention to detail and wonderfully calm, kind ways are a daily example to me. I'm sure Sue thought this book was just another celebrity vehicle, but as we sat together talking food for hours and hours while her ancient tape recorder chugged along, she recognised that the book was inside me and I realised that writing about my food journey was a good idea. Home cooked food matters, and no one understands that better than Sue. She is the Mary Poppins of cookery writing and I am very, very grateful for her generosity and wisdom.

Finally, as always, thanks to Ben, who tries everything and is eternally enthusiastic and encouraging; and to the boys, Orion, Hal, Bay and Oscar, who try less but have taught me so much. I love you all passionately.